T0108454

BISTRO

BISTRO

Classic French dishes to cook and enjoy at home

Laura Washburn Hutton

with photography by
Martin Brigdale

rps

RYLAND PETERS & SMALL
LONDON • NEW YORK

DESIGNER Steve Painter
EDITOR Sarah Vaughan
EDITORIAL DIRECTOR Julia Charles
HEAD OF PRODUCTION Patricia Harrington
ART DIRECTOR Leslie Harrington
PUBLISHER Cindy Richards

FOOD STYLISTS Linda Tubby & Bridget Sargeson
PROP STYLIST Helen Trent
INDEXER Hilary Bird

Originally published in 2010 as *The French Country Table* by Laura Washburn Hutton. This updated edition published in 2020 by Ryland Peters & Small
20–21 Jockey's Fields
London WC1R 4BW

www.rylandpeters.com

10 9 8 7 6 5 4 3 2 1

Text © Laura Washburn Hutton 2010, 2020
Design and photographs © Ryland Peters & Small 2010, 2020

Printed in China

ISBN: 978-1-78879-282-0

A CIP record for this book is available from the British Library.

US Library of Congress CIP Data has been applied for.

NOTES
• Both British (Metric) and American (Imperial plus US cup) measurements are included in these recipes for your convenience, however it is important to work with one set of measurements and not alternate between the two within a recipe.
• All spoon measurements are level, unless otherwise specified.
• All herbs are fresh unless specified as dried.
• All eggs are medium (UK) or large (US), unless specified as large, in which case US extra-large should be used. It is generally recommended that free-range eggs be used. Uncooked or partially cooked eggs should not be served to the very young, the very old, those with compromised immune systems, or to pregnant women.
• When a recipe calls for the grated zest of citrus fruit, buy unwaxed fruit and wash well before using. If you can only find treated fruit, scrub well in warm soapy water and rinse before using.
• Ovens should be preheated to the specified temperatures. If you are using a fan-assisted oven, adjust temperatures according to the manufacturer's instructions.

Contents

Introduction

The cuisine of France is exceptional. It is based on local ingredients and regional recipes, and a great deal of respect for tradition. Many of the ingredients in French cuisine can be found most anywhere in the world: garden-fresh vegetables like green beans, tomatoes, potatoes and herbs; poultry, lamb and beef are prominent; the coastlines offer an abundance of seafood, and the tradition of French cheese-making is world renowned. So what is it they do with these kitchen basics that makes their cuisine stand out from the rest?

One essential ingredient is simplicity. French cuisine suffers from a misconception that it is complicated, but the best French food is inherently straightforward. 'Faites simple' (keep it simple) is the advice given centuries ago by one of the greatest French chefs of all time, Auguste Escoffier. To my mind, this represents the essence of French cuisine. It's not elaborate, it's everyday food for ordinary people.

Another vital component is time. The French take time for food. They take time to produce it, to shop for it and to prepare it but, mostly, they take the time to eat it. And this is one thing we all have. Even in a busy world, even on a budget, time is there for the taking.

The collection of recipes in this book is a testament to the glory of French food, in all its simplicity. Nothing fancy, nothing complicated. And if you feel pressed for time in this busy world, think again. Simple food is often fast food.

The recipes in this book are also a collection of memories, of the things that made life different and special when I first lived in France. Not only did I learn to cook there, I learned to enjoy food. And I came to appreciate the rituals around food: the transferring of family recipes from one generation to the next, shopping at the market and spending most of Sunday afternoon eating lunch.

When I think back, the most pleasurable experience occurred before I even got into the kitchen; I loved shopping for food. Of course, we bought items at the supermarket, but this was usually basics and staples. The important things were bought at the market, or from speciality shops like cheese from the fromager, fresh bread from the boulangerie or sausage from the traiteur.

After I finished cooking school, I began to work for Patricia Wells. At the time, she lived near one of Paris's best street markets, which meant I had the good fortune of passing through each day on the way home, with a head full of ideas for dinner after a day spent researching, editing and translating recipes. I got to know the people who sold me the food, often by name, and they got to know my preferences. When truffle season started, Monsieur Claude from the traiteur shop always made sure to keep one very small truffle just for me. And he taught me that if I kept it for a few weeks in an a well-sealed jar of very good short-grain rice (which he also sold me!), the rice would take on the flavours and I could use it for truffle-scented risotto.

I've always liked to eat, but France taught me to love food. I learned to respect the quality of ingredients, and the skill of the people who produce such things, and I discovered that where something was grown, and even how, mattered. I loved the way each day there was constructed around a meal as if nothing else could possibly be more important than food.

Fortunately, the pleasure of cooking and eating like I did in France is a memory I can keep alive, and share, no matter where in the world I am.

Appetizers

Rustic pâté with green peppercorns

Terrine de campagne au poivre vert

If you've never made your own terrine, try this. It is simplicity itself, and you may never use shop-bought pâtés again. If you ask your butcher to grind all the meat, except the liver, then it will be even easier. Serve in slices to begin an informal meal, with plenty of fresh baguette, unsalted butter and French cornichons. It also makes a great sandwich filling.

250 g/1 lb. boneless pork shoulder, minced/ground

250 g/1 lb. pork belly, minced/ground

500 g/2 lb. veal, minced/ground

200 g/8 oz. calves' liver, finely chopped

1 egg, beaten

2 shallots, finely chopped

2 garlic cloves, crushed

1 tablespoon coarse sea salt

freshly ground black pepper

2 tablespoons green peppercorns in brine, drained, plus extra for decorating

½ teaspoon ground allspice

3 tablespoons Cognac

a handful of fresh bay leaves (see method)

To serve

French cornichons

unsalted butter

sliced baguette

a rectangular terrine mould, 30 x 11 cm/ 12 x 14 inches

baking parchment

Serves 10–12

Preheat the oven to 180°C (350°F) Gas 4.

Put the pork shoulder and belly, veal and liver in a large bowl. Add the egg, shallots, garlic, salt, pepper, green peppercorns, allspice and Cognac and mix well, preferably with your hands.

Fill the mould with the meat mixture, patting to spread evenly. Arrange the bay leaves on top of the mould and dot with extra green peppercorns. Set it in a roasting pan and add enough boiling water to come half-way up the sides of the mould. Cover the terrine with foil and bake in the preheated oven for about 1½ hours, until a knife inserted in the middle is hot to the touch after 30 seconds.

Remove from the oven and let cool. When the terrine is at room temperature, cover with baking parchment and weight with a few food cans. Refrigerate, with the weights on top. Leave for at least 1 day, but 3 days is best. The pâté will keep, refrigerated, for 1 week. Bring to room temperature before serving.

Mackerel pâté Rillettes de maquereaux

Rillettes, a coarse but spreadable pâté, is normally made from pork or goose. This is a lighter version, made from mackerel poached in white wine, giving it a pleasant, almost pickled taste. Serve this straight from the bowl, passing it around the table at the start of an informal gathering, or spread it on crackers and serve with drinks. There's no point making this in small batches — but it freezes well, in case this is more than you need, or if you have leftovers.

2 fresh mackerel, about 400 g/ 14 oz. each, well cleaned, with heads on

1 onion, sliced

40 g/3 tablespoons unsalted butter, cut into pieces and melted or softened

a large handful of flat-leaf parsley

a few sprigs of tarragon, leaves stripped

freshly squeezed juice of 1 lemon

a dash of Tabasco

coarse sea salt and freshly ground black pepper

Court bouillon

1 carrot, sliced

1 onion, sliced

1 lemon, sliced

1 sprig of thyme

1 fresh bay leaf

a few black peppercorns

1 clove

750 ml/3¼ cups dry white wine

2 teaspoons salt

To serve

toast or sliced baguette
lemon wedges

Serves 6—8

One day before serving, put all the court bouillon ingredients in a saucepan. Bring to the boil over high heat, boil for 1 minute, then cover and simmer gently for 20 minutes.

Preheat the oven to 150°C (300°F) Gas 2. Make 3 slits in the mackerels on either side, to help the flavours to penetrate the flesh. Put them in a large baking dish and pour over the hot court bouillon. Cook in the preheated oven for 30 minutes. Let cool in the liquid, then cover and refrigerate overnight.

The day of serving, remove the mackerel from the dish and lift the fillets, removing as many bones as possible.

Put the fillets, and most of the onion, in a food processor. Add the butter, parsley and tarragon and blend briefly. Transfer to a serving bowl and stir in the lemon juice, Tabasco and a generous grinding of pepper. Taste and adjust the seasoning.

Refrigerate until firm, then serve with toast or sliced baguette and lemon wedges for squeezing.

On a visit to France, we went to the elegant seaside town of Hossegor. We window-shopped around the centre, then strolled through the back streets, trying to choose which villa we would buy when we won the lottery. By the time we got to the seafront, we were famished. The first restaurant we saw had chipirons à l'ail written on the blackboard so we sat down, ordered some, and had a most memorable meal. Chipirons are tiny squid, very sweet and delicate, and were unavailable where I lived at the time, but prawns/shrimp are a good substitute. Serve with lots of bread to mop up the garlicky sauce.

Garlic prawns Crevettes à l'ail

125 ml/½ cup olive oil

1 kg/2 lbs. prawn/shrimp tails, with shells

8–10 garlic cloves, chopped

a large handful of flat-leaf parsley, chopped

coarse sea salt and freshly ground black pepper

lemon wedges, to serve

Serves 4

Heat the oil in a large frying pan/skillet. When hot but not smoking, add the prawns/shrimp and garlic and cook for 3–5 minutes, until the prawns/shrimp turn pink. Be careful not to let the garlic burn.

Remove from the heat, sprinkle with salt, freshly ground black pepper and parsley and mix well. Serve immediately, with plenty of lemon wedges on the side for squeezing.

Crudités

Crudités are a classic appetizer, especially in Parisian cafés and bistros, and they are a favourite of mine. The combination of ingredients given is fairly representative, but it does vary. Canned sweetcorn and tuna are common, as are hard-boiled/cooked eggs. You could quite easily make a meal of this by increasing the quantities or adding other ingredients to make it more elegant and contemporary. Try quails' eggs, sliced cherry tomatoes, peeled blanched broad/fava beans or wafer-thin red onion slices.

2 tablespoons wine vinegar

¼ red cabbage, thinly sliced

250 g/8 oz. baby new potatoes

200 g/7 oz. fresh asparagus spears
or fine green beans

3 medium carrots, grated

1 tablespoon freshly squeezed
lemon juice

3 cooked beetroot/beets

1 medium cucumber

a handful of flat-leaf parsley,
finely chopped

fine sea salt

1 baguette, sliced, to serve

Vinaigrette

3 tablespoons wine vinegar

1 teaspoon fine sea salt

2 teaspoons Dijon mustard

10 tablespoons sunflower oil

freshly ground black pepper

Serves 4

To make the vinaigrette, put the vinegar in a bowl. Using a fork or a small wire whisk, stir in the salt until almost dissolved. Mix in the mustard until completely blended. Add the oil, 1 tablespoon at a time, whisking/beating well between each addition, until emulsified. Add pepper to taste. Set aside.

Heat the vinegar in a saucepan. As soon as it boils, remove from the heat, add the red cabbage and toss well. Salt lightly and set aside until the cabbage turns an even deep, fuchsia colour.

Meanwhile, put the potatoes in a saucepan with sufficient cold water to cover. Bring to the boil, add salt and cook for about 15 minutes, until tender. Drain, peel and slice thinly.

Bring another saucepan of water to the boil. Add the asparagus and cook for 3–5 minutes, until just tender. Drain and set aside.

Put the carrots, lemon juice and a pinch of salt in a bowl and toss well; set aside. Cut the beetroot/beets in quarters lengthways, then slice thinly to get small triangular pieces. Peel the cucumber, cut it in quarters lengthways and slice.

Arrange small mounds of each ingredient on plates, alternating colours. Add a few spoonfuls of vinaigrette to each one and sprinkle with parsley. Serve with a basket of sliced baguette.

Goats' cheese tart Tarte au chèvre

Unlike most dishes cooked with cheese, this is very light and elegant, perfect to serve before a rich stew. It is also very moreish and you could be tempted to make a meal of it with a simple green salad. Alternatively, you could make individual tarts for a picnic, buffet or dinner party. Serve with a white wine from the Loire.

200 g/1½ cups plain/
    all-purpose flour,
    plus extra for dusting
100 g/7 tablespoons cold
    unsalted butter, cut into
    pieces
a pinch of salt
3–4 tablespoons cold water

Goats' cheese filling

3 eggs
200 ml/¾ cup crème fraîche
    or sour cream
3 Crottin de Chavignol goats'
    cheeses, about 50–75 g/
    2–3 oz. each
50 g/2 oz. Gruyère cheese,
    finely grated
a small bunch of chives,
    snipped
fine sea salt

*baking parchment and baking
    weights or dried beans*
*a loose-based tart pan,
    27 cm/11 inches diameter*

Serves 4—6

To make the pastry, put the flour, butter and salt in a food processor and, using the pulse button, process until the butter is broken down (about 5–10 pulses). Add 3 tablespoons cold water and pulse just until the mixture forms coarse crumbs; add 1 more tablespoon if necessary, but do not do more than 10 pulses.

Transfer the pastry to a sheet of baking parchment, form into a ball and flatten to a disc. Wrap in parchment paper and refrigerate for 30–60 minutes.

Roll out the pastry on a flour-dusted work surface to a disc slightly larger than the tart pan. Carefully transfer the pastry to the pan, patching any holes as you go and pressing gently into the sides. To trim the edges, roll a rolling pin over the top, using the edge of the pan as a cutting surface and let the excess fall away. Tidy up the edges and refrigerate for about 30–60 minutes, until firm.

Preheat the oven to 200°C (400°F) Gas 6. Prick the pastry all over, line with baking parchment and fill with baking weights. Bake in the preheated oven for 15 minutes, then remove the paper and weights and bake for 10–15 minutes more, until just golden. Let the tart shell cool slightly before filling. Leave the oven on.

To make the filling, put the eggs, crème fraîche or sour cream and a large pinch of salt in a bowl and whisk/beat well. Slice each goats' cheese into 3 rounds and arrange in the tart shell. Pour in the egg mixture and sprinkle with the Gruyère. Sprinkle the chives over the top.

Bake in the still hot oven for 20–30 minutes, until browned. Serve warm with leafy salad greens.

Soups

Soupe au pistou

This recipe is a staple of Provençal cuisine. Purists will tell you that aged Gouda is imperative. The reason, according to one story, is that this soup was invented by Italian workers building the railway in the hills above Nice, who used the Dutch cheese because there was a lot of it in transit at the port.

3 tablespoons olive oil

1 onion, chopped

1 small fennel bulb, quartered, cored and chopped

2 courgettes/zucchini, chopped

200 g/8 oz. new potatoes, chopped

2 tomatoes, skinned, deseeded and chopped

2 litres/quarts vegetable or chicken stock

a sprig of thyme

400-g/14-oz. can cannellini beans, drained

400-g/14-oz. can kidney beans, drained

150 g/6 oz. green beans, cut into 3-cm/1-inch pieces

50 g/2 oz. spaghetti, broken into pieces

150 g/1⅔ cups finely grated cheese (aged Gouda or Parmesan)

coarse sea salt and freshly ground black pepper

Pistou

6 garlic cloves

leaves from a small bunch of basil

6 tablespoons extra virgin olive oil

Serves 4—6

Heat the oil in a large saucepan/pot or casserole dish. Add the onion, fennel and courgettes/zucchini and cook over medium heat for about 10 minutes, until browned. Add the potatoes, tomatoes, stock and thyme. Bring to the boil, then cover and simmer gently for 15 minutes.

Add the cannellini and kidney beans and simmer, covered, for 15 minutes more. Taste and adjust the seasoning. Add the green beans and the spaghetti and cook for about 10 minutes more, until the pasta is tender. Cover and let stand. Ideally, the soup should rest for at least a few hours before serving, or make one day in advance and refrigerate. (Do not make the pistou until you are ready to serve; it is best fresh, and the basil and garlic should not be cooked.)

To make the pistou, put the garlic, basil and oil in a small food processor and blend until well chopped. You can also make it using a mortar and pestle, starting with the garlic and finishing with the oil, added gradually. It is more authentic, but I've never been very good at this method.

To serve, heat the soup and pass round the pistou and cheese, to be stirred in to taste. The soup can also be served at room temperature.

A classic case of less is more. This soup is soothing and restorative, and deliciously delicate, despite its rustic origins. Home-made salt pork makes all the difference to the taste and is very simple to make. If you don't have time to salt the pork yourself, buy a smoked pork knuckle from the butcher and proceed as in the main recipe. Your butcher should also be able to supply the pickling salt.

Cabbage soup Soupe au chou

750 g/1½ lbs. pork belly, sliced

100 g/4 oz. pickling salt

1 onion, studded with a clove

1 fresh bay leaf

1 cabbage

1 inner celery stick/stalk with leaves, cut into chunks

7 carrots, cut into chunks

4 turnips, cut into chunks

1 tablespoon unsalted butter, plus more for serving

750 g/1¾ lbs. small new potatoes, peeled

coarse sea salt

Serves 4—6

Three days before you plan to serve the soup, put the pork belly slices in a shallow non-reactive dish and add water to cover. Add the salt and stir until dissolved. Cover and refrigerate for 3 days, turning occasionally.

The day of serving, remove the pork belly from its brine and rinse. Put the pork and onion in a large saucepan/pot with 3 litres/quarts water. Bring to the boil and skim off any foam that rises to the surface, then reduce the heat, cover and let simmer.

Meanwhile, bring another saucepan of water to the boil with a bay leaf. When it boils, add the cabbage and blanch for 5 minutes. Remove the cabbage and drain. When cool enough to handle, slice the cabbage.

Add the sliced cabbage, celery, carrots, turnips and butter to the pork. Taste for seasoning; it may not need any salt because of the salt pork. Return to the boil, then lower the heat, cover and simmer for about 30 minutes.

Add the potatoes and cook for 20–25 minutes, until tender. To serve, remove the pork belly and cut into bite-sized pieces. Trim off any rind and discard any bones. Return the pork pieces to the soup and serve hot, with a spoonful of butter in each bowl and thick slices of country bread.

Kitchen garden soup Soupe du potager

An old-fashioned nourishing soup, full of healthy green things. If you do not have sorrel growing in your garden (or available in your supermarket), it can be omitted.

1 fresh bay leaf
1 small cabbage, quartered
60 g/4 tablespoons unsalted butter
2 leeks, halved and sliced
1 onion, chopped
2 teaspoons fine sea salt
250 g/8 oz. new potatoes, chopped
a handful of flat-leaf parsley, chopped
250 g/2 cups fresh shelled peas
1 Little Gem/Bibb lettuce, quartered and sliced thinly
a bunch of sorrel, sliced
unsalted butter and/or crème fraîche, to serve (optional)
sea salt and freshly ground black pepper

Serves 4—6

Put the bay leaf in a large saucepan/pot of water and bring to the boil. Add the cabbage quarters and blanch for 3 minutes. Drain the cabbage, pat dry and slice it thinly.

Heat the butter in a large saucepan/pot. Add the cabbage, leeks, onion and 2 teaspoons salt and cook for 5–10 minutes, until softened. Add the potatoes, parsley and 2 litres water. Add more salt and pepper to taste and simmer gently for 40 minutes.

Stir in the peas, lettuce and sorrel and cook for 10 minutes more. Taste for seasoning. Ladle into bowls, add 1 tablespoon of butter and/or crème fraîche, if using, to each and serve.

Vegetable bouillabaisse   Bouillabaisse borgne

It is difficult to make true bouillabaisse outside France because so many of the fish used are found only in the Mediterranean. But here's a very good vegetable-only alternative, with all the same flavours, including the best part – the chilli/chile-spiked rouille sauce. Traditional versions include a poached egg, which I have omitted.

4 tablespoons olive oil

2 leeks, white part only, halved lengthways, then sliced crossways

1 large onion, coarsely chopped

1 fennel bulb, halved, cored and chopped

3 garlic cloves, crushed

3 large ripe tomatoes, skinned, deseeded and chopped

5 medium new potatoes, cubed

2 litres/quarts vegetable stock or water

1 fresh bay leaf

a sprig of thyme

a strip of peel from 1 unwaxed orange

1 teaspoon good-quality saffron threads

1 baguette loaf, sliced, for croûtons

100 g/1½ cups freshly grated Gruyère cheese

coarse sea salt and freshly ground black pepper

a handful of chopped flat-leaf parsley, to serve

Rouille

3 garlic cloves, very finely chopped

1–2 red chillies/chiles, deseeded and very finely chopped

1 egg yolk, at room temperature

about 300 ml/1¼ cups extra virgin olive oil

sea salt and freshly ground black pepper

Serves 4–6

Heat the oil in a large saucepan/pot. Add the leeks, onions and fennel and cook for about 10 minutes, until just beginning to brown. Stir in the garlic, tomatoes, potatoes and 1 teaspoon salt and cook for 1 minute. Add the stock, bay leaf, thyme, orange peel and saffron and stir. Bring to the boil, reduce the heat and simmer gently for about 40 minutes, until the potatoes are tender. Add salt and pepper to taste, cover and let stand for at least 1 hour, or let cool and refrigerate overnight.

Before you serve, make the croûtons. Preheat the oven to 180°C (350°F) Gas 4. Arrange the baguette slices in a single layer on a baking sheet. Bake in the preheated oven for about 5–8 minutes, until golden. Set aside.

To make the rouille, put the garlic, chillies/chiles and egg yolk in a small, deep bowl. Beat well. Add the oil a little at a time and beating vigorously, until the mixture is thick like mayonnaise. Season to taste with salt and pepper.

To serve, warm the soup if necessary. Put 2–3 croûtons in each soup plate, sprinkle with the grated cheese and ladle in the soup. Sprinkle with chopped parsley and serve with the rouille, to be stirred in according to taste.

French onion soup

Soupe gratinée à l'oignon

Although this soup is synonymous with bistro eating, it is also associated with another tradition. At French weddings, especially in the countryside, it was often served in the early hours of the morning, as a restorative after a long night of celebrating. This recipe is a simplified version, the sort of thing that's ideal when it's chilly outside, people are hungry inside and there's not much more than a few onions lurking about.

50 g/3 tablespoons unsalted butter

1 tablespoon olive oil

3 large onions, about 1.3 kg/3 lbs., thinly sliced

2 garlic cloves, crushed

1 tablespoon plain/all-purpose flour

1 litre/quart beef, chicken or vegetable stock

600 ml/2¾ cups dry white wine

1 fresh bay leaf

2 sprigs of thyme

1 baguette, sliced

about 180 g/5 oz. Gruyère cheese, finely grated

coarse sea salt and freshly ground black pepper

Serves 4—6

Put the butter and oil in a large saucepan/pot and melt over medium heat. Add the onions and cook over low heat for 15–20 minutes, until soft.

Add the garlic and flour and cook, stirring for about 1 minute. Add the stock, wine, bay leaf and thyme. Season with salt and pepper and bring to the boil. Boil for 1 minute, then lower the heat and simmer very gently for 20 minutes. Taste and adjust the seasoning. At this point, the soup will be cooked, but standing time will improve the flavour – at least 30 minutes.

Before serving, preheat the grill/broiler. Put the baguette slices on a baking sheet and brown under the grill/broiler until lightly toasted. Set aside. Do not turn the grill/broiler off.

To serve, ladle the soup into ovenproof bowls and top with a few toasted baguette rounds. Sprinkle grated cheese over the top and cook under the still hot grill/broiler until browned and bubbling. Serve immediately.

Basque fish soup Ttoro

France has many fish soups but only this one includes hot chillies/chiles. Another plus is that it can be made successfully without hard-to-come-by Mediterranean fish and, if you use good-quality fresh fish stock, it's very quick to make. The bones and prawn/shrimp shells add flavour, as well as making it a bit messy, but this is fishermen's fare, so roll up your sleeves and enjoy.

2 tablespoons olive oil

1 red (bell) pepper, halved, deseeded and sliced

1 onion, halved and sliced

3 garlic cloves, crushed

1 green chilli/chile, deseeded and chopped

¼ teaspoon hot paprika

a sprig of thyme

225 g/1 cup canned chopped tomatoes

1.5 litres/1½ quarts fresh fish stock

250 g/8 oz. monkfish fillet, cut into bite-sized pieces

500 g/1 lb. hake or cod steaks

250 g/8 oz. unpeeled prawn/shrimp tails

250 ml/1 cup dry white wine

500 g/1 lb. fresh mussels*

a handful of flat-leaf parsley, chopped

Garlic croûtons

1 baguette, sliced

2 garlic cloves, peeled

Serves 4—6

Heat the oil in a stockpot or large saucepan/pot. Add the (bell) pepper and onion and cook for about 5 minutes, until browned. Stir in the garlic, chilli/chile, paprika, thyme and tomatoes and cook for 5 minutes more.

Add the stock, monkfish, hake and prawns/shrimp. Bring to the boil, skim off the foam and simmer gently for 10–15 minutes, until the fish is cooked through.

Meanwhile, make the garlic croûtons. Preheat the oven to 180°C (350°F) Gas 4. Arrange the baguette slices in a single layer on a baking sheet. Bake in the preheated oven for 5–8 minutes, until golden. Let cool slightly, then rub with garlic cloves and set aside.

Pour the wine into a large saucepan/pot with a lid and bring to the boil for 1 minute, then remove from the heat. Add the prepared mussels to the wine, cover and steam over high heat for 2–3 minutes, just until opened. Remove the mussels from their shells, discarding any that do not open.

Add the mussels and cooking liquid to the soup and stir well. Sprinkle with parsley and serve immediately, with the garlic croûtons.

*NOTE To prepare mussels, start 15 minutes before you are ready to use. Rinse them in cold water and tap any open ones against the work surface. If they don't close, discard them. Scrub the others with a stiff brush and scrape off any barnacles. Pull off and discard the wiry beards.

Meat

Pork in cider with potatoes and apples

Porc au cidre aux deux pommes

If it has apples and cream, then it must be from Normandy. The cider is a good clue as well, and it provides a luxuriously rich sauce for the long-simmered pork. Unlike recipes from more southerly realms, this is subtle and delicate, but no less powerful for its discretion. A good dish for all the family, as children (and adults) enjoy sweet things to accompany their meat. Serve with the cider used in cooking, or a red wine from the Loire.

30 g/2 tablespoons unsalted butter

2 onions, sliced

1 tablespoon sunflower oil

1 pork middle leg roast, about
     1.75 kg/3½ lbs.

1.5 litres/1½ quarts dry cider

2 sprigs of thyme

800 g/1¾ lbs. new potatoes,
     peeled and halved lengthways

125 ml/½ cup double/heavy cream

coarse sea salt and freshly
     ground black pepper

Apples

60 g/4 tablespoons unsalted butter

5 tart apples, such as Braeburn or
     Cox's, peeled, cored and sliced

a large flameproof casserole dish

Serves 4

Preheat the oven to 150°C (300°F) Gas 2.

Melt the butter in a large flameproof casserole dish. Add the onions and cook gently for about 5 minutes, until softened but not browned. Remove the onions. Add the oil, increase the heat, add the pork and cook until browned all over. Remove and season well with salt and pepper.

Add some of the cider to the casserole dish, heat and scrape the bottom of the pan. Return the meat, onions, remaining cider and thyme. Season lightly and bring to the boil. Boil for 1 minute, skim off any foam that rises to the surface, then reduce the heat, cover and cook in the preheated oven for 4 hours. Turn the pork regularly and taste and adjust the seasoning half-way through the cooking time.

One hour before the end of the cooking time, add the potatoes and continue cooking.

Remove from the oven, transfer the pork and potatoes to a plate and cover with foil to keep it warm. Cook the sauce over high heat for 10–15 minutes to reduce slightly. Taste and adjust the seasoning.

Meanwhile, to cook the apples, melt the butter in a large frying pan/skillet, add the apples and cook over high heat for 5–10 minutes, until browned and tender. Do not crowd the pan; use 2 pans if necessary.

To serve, slice the pork and arrange on plates with the potatoes and apples. Stir the cream into the sauce and serve immediately.

Pork chops with piquant sauce Côtes de porc charcutière

This is the sort of basic fare you'll find in cafés and bistros all over France. The mustardy-vinegary sauce is ideal with pork. Cornichons are the best part so be sure to use the real thing. They must be small and, ideally, bottled in France. I've seen other tiny gherkins labelled as cornichons but, unless they come from France, they never taste as I expect. Serve with mashed potatoes.

4 thick-cut pork chops, rind removed

extra virgin olive oil

coarse sea salt and freshly ground black pepper

Piquant sauce

60 ml/¼ cup wine, dry white or red

250 ml/1 cup fresh chicken stock

60 ml/¼ cup tarragon or sherry vinegar

40 g/4 tablespoons unsalted butter

3 shallots, finely chopped

1 tablespoon plain/all-purpose flour

2 teaspoons tomato purée/paste

1 teaspoon coarse Dijon mustard

8 French cornichons, sliced into rounds

a sprig of tarragon, leaves stripped and chopped

a small handful of flat-leaf parsley, chopped

a ridged stove-top grill pan

Serves 2—4

To make the sauce, put the wine and stock in a small saucepan. Bring to the boil for 1 minute, then stir in the vinegar. Set aside.

Melt the butter in another saucepan. Add the shallots and cook for 3–5 minutes, until soft. Add the flour and cook, stirring for 1 minute. Add the warm stock mixture and tomato purée/paste and mix well. Simmer gently for 15 minutes.

Meanwhile, to cook the pork chops, rub a ridged stove-top grill pan with the oil and heat on high. When hot, add the pork chops and cook for 4–5 minutes. Turn and cook the other side for 3–4 minutes. Remove from the heat and season on both sides with salt and pepper.

Stir the mustard, cornichons, tarragon and parsley into the sauce and serve immediately, with the pork chops and plenty of mashed potatoes.

If you thought pork was bland, think again. It is actually a spectacular vehicle for all sorts of flavours and responds remarkably well to marinating. The French have known this for years, because the idea for this recipe came from one of my favourite cookbooks, La Cuisine de Mme Saint-Ange, first published in 1927. Any cut of pork can be marinated, from a few hours to overnight, and the leftovers are as good, if not better, than the original. Serve with something creamy, like the Cauliflower Gratin (page 115), or some mashed potatoes.

Marinated pork roast   Côti de porc mariné

1 boneless pork loin roast,
   about 1.5 kg/3 lbs.

1 large onion, sliced

2 carrots, sliced

1 celery stick/stalk, with leaves

2–3 tablespoons crème fraîche

Marinade

750 ml/3¼ cups dry white wine

3 tablespoons white wine vinegar

2 garlic cloves, peeled and sliced

1 fresh bay leaf

2–3 fresh sage leaves

a sprig of thyme

2 tablespoons coarse sea salt

1 tablespoon sugar

1 teaspoon black peppercorns

a roasting pan with a lid

Serves 4—6

One day (or about 8–12 hours) before serving, mix all the ingredients for the marinade together in a large non-reactive bowl. Add the pork and vegetables, cover and refrigerate, turning the pork once or twice.

When ready to cook, preheat the oven to 200°C (400°F) Gas 6. Remove the pork from the marinade and put it in a roasting pan with a lid which holds it snugly. Roast for 30 minutes.

Lower the heat to 170°C (320°F) Gas 3. Add the vegetables and all the marinade ingredients. Add some water if necessary so the pork is just covered. Continue to cook, covered, for 1½ hours, basting occasionally with the marinating liquid.

To serve, remove the meat from the cooking liquid, set aside and keep warm. Taste the cooking liquid and add 1 more tablespoon vinegar if it needs acidity. Bring the sauce to a boil and reduce for 15 minutes. Stir in the crème fraîche. Taste and adjust the seasoning.

Arrange the pork on a serving dish and pour over the sauce and vegetables.

Cassoulet

A classic from the south-west, adapted for those of us outside France. Do not let the long list put you off. This is actually quite easy: cook the beans, cook the meat stew, brown the duck and sausages, then put it all together. That's it. You do need good sausages, with as high a pork content as possible. Duck confit is sold canned in large supermarkets, or in good delicatessens. You will also need several large pots, a large dish to cook it in and very hungry friends.

Beans

850 g/1¾ lbs. dried haricot beans

300 g/10 oz. thick-sliced unsmoked middle bacon/country ham

rind from 4 thick pork chops/ piece of salt pork

1 carrot, chopped

1 fresh bay leaf

1 onion, studded with 2 cloves

4 whole garlic cloves

1 teaspoon salt

Meat

1 tablespoon olive oil

750 g/1½ lbs. pork spare ribs

750 g/1½ lbs. boneless lamb shoulder, cubed

1 onion, chopped

3 garlic cloves, crushed

400 g/2 cups canned chopped tomatoes

1 fresh bay leaf

2 litres/quarts fresh chicken stock

6 canned duck confit thigh pieces

10 Toulouse sausages or other pure pork sausages

150 g/1 cup fresh breadcrumbs

coarse sea salt and freshly ground black pepper

a large casserole dish

Serves 8

In the morning, one day before serving, put the beans in a bowl with plenty of cold water and let soak (soak for at least 6 hours, or start 2 days early and soak overnight).

Drain the beans. Put in a large saucepan/pot with cold water to cover, bring to the boil and simmer for 10 minutes. Drain. Return the beans to the pan and add the bacon, pork rind, carrot, bay leaf, onion and garlic. Cover with water by about 5 cm/2 inches and bring to the boil. Lower the heat and simmer gently for 1 hour. Add 1 teaspoon salt and continue cooking for 30 minutes more. Let cool, then refrigerate overnight; do not drain.

Meanwhile, to prepare the meat stew, heat the oil in a large frying pan/ skillet. Add the pork and lamb and fry until brown. Add the onion and garlic and cook for about 3 minutes, until just soft. Add the tomatoes, bay leaf and stock. Season. Bring to the boil, skim off the foam, then lower the heat, cover and simmer gently for 1½ hours. Add salt and pepper to taste. Let cool, cover and refrigerate overnight.

The next day, about 3 hours before serving, discard the fat from the top of the stew. Remove the meat from the spare ribs, return to the stew and discard the bones. Bring the beans to room temperature (or warm slightly), drain and reserve the liquid. Season to taste.

Heat a large frying pan/skillet, add the duck confit pieces and fry until browned. Remove, cut the thighs into pieces and set aside. In the same pan, brown the sausages. Do not discard the cooking fat.

Preheat the oven to 220°C (425°F) Gas 7. Now you are ready to assemble. Remove the pork rind and bacon from the beans and put in a large casserole dish. Top with one-third of the beans. Arrange the duck confit in the middle (so that you know where to find it when serving), and the sausages all around the edge. Spread the meat stew on top. Cover with the remaining beans. Spoon in some of the reserved bean liquid (you should just be able to see it), then sprinkle with a thin layer of breadcrumbs. Pour in the duck and sausage fat. Cook in the preheated oven for 30 minutes.

Reduce the oven temperature to 190°C (375°F) Gas 5. Gently break up the crust on top, then spoon over some more bean liquid and sprinkle with more breadcrumbs. Continue checking, about every 30 minutes or so, adding more liquid as necessary; be sure not to let the cassoulet dry out. When the cassoulet has cooked for 2 hours and the crust is well browned, remove from the oven.

Serve hot, allowing a portion of confit, the sausages and plenty of beans for each person.

Steak and frites

Steak frites

Nothing says 'bistro' better than this. The shallot butter is a fancy flourish; it is just as authentic to serve as is, with nothing more than Dijon mustard, for both the steak and the frites (but no ketchup, please!) The secret of cooking great frites is to use a good floury variety of potato and to cook them twice. They should be dry, rustling, crisp and well seasoned.

4 sirloin or rib eye steaks, about 300 g/
 10 oz. each, 3 cm/1 inch thick

1 tablespoon sunflower oil

coarse sea salt and freshly
 ground black pepper

Shallot butter

100 g/1 stick unsalted butter,
 softened

2 shallots, finely chopped

150 ml/⅔ cup red wine

a large sprig of tarragon

several sprigs of flat-leaf parsley

1 teaspoon coarse sea salt

½ teaspoon freshly ground
 black pepper

Frites

500 g/1 lb. floury potatoes

sunflower oil, for deep frying

sea salt, to serve

*a large saucepan/pot with
 frying basket*

a ridged stove-top grill pan

Serves 4

To make the shallot butter, put about 25 g/¼ stick of the butter in a saucepan and melt over low heat. Add the shallots and cook until softened. Add the wine, bring to the boil and cook until syrupy and the wine has almost completely evaporated. Set aside to cool.

Put the cooled shallots, remaining butter, tarragon, parsley, salt and pepper in a small food processor and blend briefly. Transfer the mixture to a piece of baking parchment and shape into a log. Roll up and chill until firm.

To prepare the frites, peel the potatoes and cut into 5 mm/¼-inch slices. Cut the slices into 5 mm/¼-inch strips. Put into a bowl of iced water for 5 minutes. When ready to cook, drain and pat dry with kitchen paper/paper towels.

Fill a large saucepan/pot one-third full with oil. Heat the oil to 190°C (375°F) or until a cube of bread browns in 30 seconds. Working in batches, put 2 large handfuls of potato strips into the frying basket, lower carefully into the oil and fry for about 4 minutes. Remove and drain on kitchen paper/paper towels. Repeat until all the strips have been cooked. Skim any debris off the top of the oil, reheat to the same temperature, then fry the strips for a second time (about 2 minutes), until crisp and golden. Remove and drain on kitchen paper/paper towels, then sprinkle with salt. Keep hot in the oven until ready to serve.

To prepare the steaks, rub them on both sides with the oil. Heat a ridged stove-top grill pan until hot. Cook the steaks for just 1½–2 minutes. Turn and cook the other side for 1–2 minutes. This will produce a rare steak. To produce a medium-rare steak, turn and cook again on both sides for 2–3 minutes more. Remove from the pan and season both sides. Let stand for a few minutes. Serve with rounds of the shallot butter and the hot frites.

Braised steak with anchovies and capers

Brouffade

The sailors who used to guide barges up and down the Rhône, from Arles to Lyon, were lucky men indeed. They invented this dish and, I assume, ate it often. If I were having my last supper, this would be it, with mashed potatoes, a green salad and a good red Rhône wine.

4 thick rump steaks, about
   300 g/10 oz. each
4 onions, halved and sliced
3 tablespoons capers, drained
12 French cornichons, chopped
10 anchovy fillets packed in oil,
   finely chopped
1 tablespoon plain/all-purpose
   flour
3 tablespoons red wine vinegar

Marinade

150 ml/⅔ cup olive oil
8 garlic cloves, crushed
a small handful of flat-leaf parsley,
   chopped
1 teaspoon coarsely ground
   black pepper
1 fresh bay leaf
a sprig of thyme
1 inner celery stick/stalk,
   with leaves

a large casserole dish

Serves 4—6

One day before serving, mix all of the marinade ingredients together in a shallow non-reactive dish. Add the steaks and turn to coat well with the mixture. Cover with clingfilm/plastic wrap and refrigerate overnight, turning at least twice.

Preheat the oven to 150°C (300°F) Gas 2.

Put the onions, capers and cornichons in a bowl and toss well. Put the anchovies and flour in a small bowl and blend well. Remove the meat from the marinade and set aside. Stir the anchovies and vinegar into the marinade.

Put one-third of the onion mixture in the casserole dish and put 2 steaks on top, side by side. Spoon in half of the marinade, spreading it over the meat. Top with half the remaining onion mixture, then the remaining steaks. Spoon over the rest of the marinade and top with the rest of the onion mixture.

Pour in about 250 ml/1 cup water. Cut a piece of baking parchment to about the diameter of the casserole dish and put this on top of the onions to help seal in all the juices. Cover with the lid and cook in the preheated oven for 3 hours. Serve immediately with mashed potatoes and salad greens.

Braised beef brisket with carrots

Boeuf aux carottes

This humble French culinary masterpiece rates high on the scale of life's little pleasures. It has no precise geographical origin – everyone makes it, and rightly so. The beef practically melts in your mouth and the broth is rich, sweet and buttery from all the carrots. A prime candidate for potatoes, tagliatelle or, even better, the Macaroni Gratin (page 91). French Beans with Garlic (page 110) would also be delicious. Experiment with different cuts of beef – anything that will stand up to long, slow simmering.

2 tablespoons olive oil

1.5 kg/3 lbs. rolled and tied beef brisket

1.5 kg/3 lbs. carrots

150 g/6 oz. bacon lardons

1 onion, halved and sliced

2 garlic cloves, crushed

1 fresh bay leaf

a sprig of thyme

1 small leafy celery stick/stalk

500 ml/2 cups dry white wine

coarse sea salt and freshly ground black pepper

a large flameproof casserole dish

Serves 4—6

Preheat the oven to 150°C (300°F) Gas 2.

Heat 1 tablespoon of the oil in a large flameproof casserole dish. Add the meat and cook until browned on all sides. Transfer to a plate and sprinkle generously with salt.

Heat the remaining oil in the casserole dish, add the carrots and 1 teaspoon salt and cook for 3–5 minutes, stirring occasionally, until brown. Remove and set aside.

Put the lardons and onion in the casserole dish and cook over high heat for 3–5 minutes, until browned.

Add the garlic, bay leaf, thyme, celery, carrots and beef. Pour in the wine and add water almost to cover. Bring to the boil, skim, then cover with a lid and cook in the preheated oven for 3 hours. Turn the meat over at least once during cooking.

Sprinkle with pepper and serve with your choice of accompaniments.

Stuffed tomatoes

Tomates farcies

This classic dish is a reminder that good French food is not about expensive cuts, or elaborate sauces. In fact, the real recipe calls for leftover beef from a stew – home economy at its best. If you have any leftovers from the Braised Beef Brisket (page 48), then use them. It's also nice if you mix leftovers, like lamb and pork, with the beef. This summery dish is ideal for lunch or a light supper, served with salad greens and a light-medium red wine.

2 tablespoons olive oil

4 shallots, finely chopped

3 large garlic cloves, crushed

100 g/4 oz. bacon lardons

3 tablespoons dry white wine

12 large tomatoes

375 g/13 oz. minced/ground beef

1 egg

4 tablespoons fresh breadcrumbs

½ teaspoon dried herbes de provence

a handful of flat-leaf parsley, finely chopped

coarse sea salt and freshly ground black pepper

a baking dish, greased with 2 tablespoons olive oil

Serves 4—6

Preheat the oven to 200°C (400°F) Gas 6.

Heat the oil in a large frying pan/skillet. Add the shallots and garlic and cook for 3–5 minutes, until softened but not browned. Add the bacon lardons and fry for 3–5 minutes, until just beginning to brown. Stir in the wine and cook until it has evaporated. Transfer to a large bowl and let cool.

Slice the tops off of the tomatoes and set the tops aside. Carefully deseed with a spoon. Pat the insides dry with kitchen paper/paper towels and season with salt and pepper. Set aside.

Add the beef to the shallot mixture, then stir in the egg, breadcrumbs, herbs, parsley and 1 teaspoon salt. Cook a small piece of the stuffing mixture in a frying pan/skillet, taste for seasoning, adding more salt if necessary.

Fill the tomato shells with the beef mixture, mounding it at the top. Replace the tomato tops and arrange apart in the prepared baking dish. Cook in the preheated oven for about 30 minutes, until cooked through and browned.

*VARIATION Another speciality from Provence, les petits farcis (little stuffed vegetables), can be made using the same stuffing to fill a variety of vegetables: courgettes/zucchini, aubergines/eggplant and (bell) peppers are ideal, but you can also use artichokes and mushrooms. Provençal dishes often have a breadcrumb topping, so add a handful of chopped fresh parsley, crushed garlic and some grated Parmesan to fresh breadcrumbs and sprinkle over the tops before baking.

Beef and potato gratin Hachis parmentier

Antoine-Augustin Parmentier introduced potatoes to the French public in the late 18th century, and this dish of minced/ground beef nestled between two layers of creamy mashed potatoes is a tribute to him. Not as glamorous as a bridge over the Seine perhaps, but delicious nonetheless. The traditional recipe calls for leftover cooked beef, specifically stewed or boiled beef, so use that if you have some. The taste benefits from flavourful leftovers, but minced/ground beef that has been well seasoned and cooked in a bit of wine comes close. Serve with peas or green beans and a fruity red wine.

30 g/3 tablespoons unsalted butter or 2 tablespoons sunflower oil

2 onions, chopped

2 garlic cloves

750 g/1½ lbs. minced/ground beef

70 g/3 oz. bacon, finely chopped

125 ml/½ cup dry white wine

a handful of flat-leaf parsley, chopped

a sprig of thyme, leaves stripped

2 tablespoons tomato purée/paste

50 g/¼ cup freshly grated Gruyère cheese

coarse sea salt and freshly ground black pepper

Potato purée

2 kg/4 lbs. potatoes

1 fresh bay leaf

250 ml/1 cup hot milk

100 g/1 stick unsalted butter, cut into pieces

sea salt

a baking dish, about 30 cm/ 12 inches long, greased with butter

Serves 4—6

To prepare the purée, put the potatoes and bay leaf in a saucepan of cold water. Bring to the boil, add salt and cook until tender. Drain.

Put the potatoes in a large bowl and mash coarsely with a wooden spoon. Using an electric mixer, gradually add the milk and butter, beating until the mixture is smooth. Add salt and whisk/beat well. If the potatoes are very dry, add a little more milk. Taste, then add more butter and/or salt as necessary and set aside.

Heat the butter in a frying pan/skillet, add the onions and cook over high heat for 3–5 minutes, until just brown. Add the garlic, beef and chopped bacon and cook until almost completely browned. Add the wine and cook until it has almost evaporated. Stir in the parsley, thyme leaves and tomato purée/paste. Taste and adjust the seasoning with salt and pepper.

Preheat the oven to 200°C (400°F) Gas 6.

Spread half the potatoes in the prepared baking dish. Add the beef mixture and level with a spoon. Spread with the remaining potatoes. Sprinkle with the cheese and bake in the preheated oven for about 25–30 minutes, until golden. Serve with the accompaniment of your choice.

Spring lamb stew with vegetables   Navarin d'agneau

This reminds me of long Sunday family lunches, the ones that go on almost until dinner, the likes of which I'd never known before living in France. To re-create something similar, start with apéritifs and nibbles at midday, then serve this with boiled baby new potatoes and a bottle of St-Emilion. Follow with salad greens and a generous cheese platter. A slice of the Simple Apple Tart (see page 142) before coffee makes the perfect ending. A lovely way to herald in the spring.

1 tablespoon sunflower oil

700 g/1½ lbs. lamb neck fillet, cubed

500 g/1 lb. lamb chump chops, each one cut into several pieces

1 tablespoon plain/all-purpose flour

2 ripe tomatoes, skinned, deseeded and chopped

2 garlic cloves, crushed

600 ml/2¾ cups fresh lamb or chicken stock

1 fresh bay leaf

a sprig of thyme

4 baby carrots, cut into 3-cm/1-inch pieces

200 g/8 oz. baby leeks, cut into 5-cm/2-inch lengths

200 g/8 oz. baby turnips

200 g/8 oz. sugar snap peas

a handful of flat-leaf parsley, chopped

coarse sea salt and freshly ground black pepper

a large flameproof casserole dish

Serves 4

Heat the oil in a large flameproof casserole dish. Add the lamb and brown the pieces on all sides, in batches if necessary. When all the lamb has been browned, return it all to the casserole dish, lower the heat slightly and stir in a pinch of salt and the flour. Cook, stirring to coat evenly, for 1 minute.

Add the tomatoes and garlic. Stir in the stock, bay leaf and thyme. Bring to the boil and skim off any foam that rises to the surface. Reduce the heat, then cover and simmer gently for 40 minutes.

Add the carrots, leeks and turnips and cook for 25 minutes more. Taste and adjust the seasoning with salt and pepper.

Add the sugar snap peas and cook for about 7 minutes, until tender. Sprinkle with the parsley and serve immediately.

Leg of lamb with anchovies Agneau à la gasconnade

Gasconnade refers to the anchovies and it is a traditional way of flavouring lamb in the south-west of France. The slow cooking in wine mellows the anchovies, making for a rich sauce and very tender meat. Serve with tagliatelle, potatoes or flageolet beans.

1 leg of lamb, about 1.5 kg/3 lbs., trimmed

14 anchovy fillets

2 tablespoons olive oil

2 onions, chopped

2 carrots, chopped

3 garlic cloves, crushed

2 tomatoes, skinned, deseeded and chopped

750 ml/3¼ cups red wine

2 sprigs of thyme

1 fresh bay leaf

1 tablespoon tomato purée/paste

coarse sea salt

a large flameproof casserole dish

Serves 4—6

Preheat the oven to 180°C (350°F) Gas 4.

Make slits all over the lamb and insert the anchovy fillets, as you do when studding with garlic.

Heat the oil in a large flameproof casserole dish. Add the lamb and brown on all sides. Remove, season lightly and set aside.

Put the onions and carrots in the casserole dish and cook over high heat for 3–5 minutes, until lightly browned. Add the garlic and chopped tomatoes and cook for 1 minute. Add the wine, thyme, bay leaf and tomato purée/paste and bring to the boil. Boil for 1 minute, then add the lamb.

Cover with the lid, transfer to the preheated oven and cook for 1½ hours, turning every 20 minutes or so. Remove the thyme and bay leaf and serve with the accompaniment of your choice.

Poultry and game

This poor man's version of a dish in which truffle slices are stuffed under the chicken skin makes a nice change from ordinary roast chicken. The perfume of bay leaves and thyme delicately flavours the chicken flesh, while the tartness of the lemon keeps it lively.

Roast chicken with herbs and lemon

Poulet rôti aux herbes et citron

1 free-range chicken, about
  1.5 kg/3 lbs.
2 lemons, 1 quartered, 1 sliced
6 large fresh bay leaves
2 sprigs of thyme
1–2 tablespoons olive oil or
  30 g/2 tablespoons butter
1 teaspoon dried thyme
1 onion, sliced in rounds
250 ml/1 cup dry white wine
1 tablespoon unsalted butter
coarse sea salt

a large roasting pan with a rack

Serves 4

Preheat the oven to 220°C (425°F) Gas 7.

Season the inside of the chicken generously and stuff with the lemon quarters, 2 of the bay leaves and the thyme sprigs. Using your fingers, separate the skin from the breast meat to create a pocket and put 1 bay leaf on each side of the breast, underneath the skin. Put the remaining bay leaves under the skin of the thighs. Rub the outside of the chicken all over with the oil, season generously and sprinkle over the dried thyme.

Put the chicken on its side on a rack set over a roasting pan. Add sufficient water to fill the pan by about 1 cm/½ inch and add the sliced lemon and onion. Lower the oven to 180°C (350°F) Gas 5 and cook for 45 minutes, then turn the chicken on its other side. Continue roasting the chicken for about 45 minutes more, until cooked through and the juices run clear when a thigh is pierced with a skewer. Add extra water if necessary during cooking.

Transfer the chicken to a plate, cover and let stand for 10 minutes. Add the white wine to the pan juices and cook over high heat for 3–5 minutes, scraping the bottom of the pan. Stir in the butter. Carve the chicken and serve with the pan juices.

Chicken with peppers, onions, ham and tomatoes Poulet basquaise

Like all traditional dishes, there are many versions of this recipe; some call only for green (bell) peppers, some use only onions and chillies/chilies. I think chillies/chiles are imperative, and if you want to be completely authentic, use piment d'Espelette, which is a most delicious little chilli/chile grown in the Basque region of France, but very difficult to find outside this area. They are pleasantly spicy without being overpowering, so whatever variety you use, resist the temptation to overdo it. Serve with rice.

2 tablespoons olive oil

1 free-range chicken, about
  2 kg/4 lbs., cut into 8 pieces

2 onions, sliced

2 red (bell) peppers, halved,
  deseeded and sliced

2 yellow (bell) peppers, halved,
  deseeded and sliced

2–4 large garlic cloves, crushed

2 small hot green chillies/chiles,
  deseeded and thinly sliced
  (or ½ teaspoon dried chilli/
  hot pepper flakes)

1 thick slice jambon de Bayonne
  or other unsmoked ham,
  about 2 cm/1 inch thick and
  160 g/6 oz., cut into strips

1 kg/2 lbs. ripe tomatoes, skinned,
  deseeded and chopped

coarse sea salt and freshly
  ground black pepper

Serves 4

Heat the oil in a large frying pan/skillet with a lid, add the chicken pieces skin-side down and cook for 5–10 minutes, until brown. Don't crowd the pan; if you can't fit all the pieces at once, brown in batches. Transfer the chicken to a plate, season well with salt and set aside.

Add the onions and (bell) peppers to the pan, season with salt and black pepper, then cook over medium heat for 15–20 minutes, until soft. Stir in the garlic, chillies/chiles and ham, and cook for 1 minute. Add the tomatoes, mix well, then add all the chicken pieces and bury them under the sauce.

Cover and cook over low heat for 30–40 minutes, until the chicken is tender. Serve with rice.

Chicken with tomato, garlic and olives

Poulet sauté niçoise

2 tablespoons olive oil

1 free-range chicken, about
2 kg/4 lbs., cut into 6–8 pieces

8 garlic cloves, finely chopped

400-g/14-oz can chopped tomatoes

a pinch of sugar

50 g/2 oz. black olives, preferably
niçoise, stoned/pitted and
coarsely chopped

coarse sea salt and freshly
ground black pepper

a bunch of fresh basil, torn

tagliatelle or rice, to serve

Serves 4—6

*Poulet sauté is at home all over France, but I especially like
this south-eastern version with its assertive flavours. It goes
very well with fresh pasta such as tagliatelle or rice, and
a sturdy red wine, such as a Collioure or Minervois.*

Heat 1 tablespoon of the oil in a large frying pan/skillet. Add the chicken
pieces and brown on all sides. Transfer to a plate, sprinkle generously with
salt and set aside.

Add the remaining oil and garlic to the pan and cook for 1 minute; do
not let the garlic burn. Add the tomatoes and sugar. Stir well and return the
chicken pieces to the pan. Cover and simmer gently for 25–30 minutes, until
the chicken is cooked.

Transfer the chicken pieces to a serving dish, then increase the heat and
cook the sauce for about 10 minutes, to thicken it slightly. Season to taste,
then stir in the olives. Pour the sauce over the chicken pieces, sprinkle with
the basil and serve immediately with tagliatelle or rice, as preferred.

A dish without a region, this is served pretty much all over France, in homes as well as restaurants. It's quick to make, if you get your butcher to cut up the chicken, and the flavour of tarragon lifts this out of the ordinary. Make this dish midweek and you'll have a lovely supper in under an hour, or serve it for your next dinner party and it will seem as if you slaved away all day. A red St-Estèphe or Ladoix would be the ideal wine.

Chicken with tarragon Poulet sauté à l'estragon

1 tablespoon unsalted butter

1 tablespoon sunflower oil

1 free-range corn-fed chicken, about 2 kg/4 lbs., cut into 6–8 pieces

2 carrots, chopped

1 shallot, chopped

a sprig of thyme

2–3 sprigs of flat-leaf parsley

a bunch of tarragon

3 tablespoons crème fraîche or sour cream

coarse sea salt and freshly ground black pepper

Serves 4

Melt the butter and oil in a large frying pan/skillet with a lid. Add the chicken pieces and cook for about 5 minutes, until brown. Put the browned chicken pieces on a plate and season well with salt and pepper.

Add the carrots and shallot to the pan and cook, stirring for 1–2 minutes. Return the chicken to the pan and add water to cover half-way. Add the thyme, parsley and a few sprigs of tarragon. Cover and simmer gently for 30 minutes.

Meanwhile, strip the leaves from the remaining tarragon, chop them finely and set aside. Add the stems to the cooking chicken.

Remove the chicken from the pan and put it in a serving dish. Remove and discard the tarragon stems.

Increase the heat and cook the sauce until it has reduced by half. Strain and return the sauce to the pan. Stir in the crème fraîche or sour cream and the chopped tarragon. Heat briefly (do not let it boil as the cream will split) and pour over the chicken. Serve immediately.

Guinea fowl with lentils Pintade aux lentilles

If you can find a true guinea fowl, from a butcher or specialist supplier, then it will taste as it should. It is worth the effort to search out the real thing because supermarket guinea fowl is disappointing, to say the least. The flavour bears no resemblance to anything worth paying money for; you are better off buying an organic or free-range chicken, since the preparation is the same and the result will be superior. Fortunately, the lentils will never disappoint.

1 guinea fowl, about 1.5 kg/3 lbs.

3 tablespoons olive oil

225 g/1 cup dried green lentils, preferably French

a sprig of thyme

1 fresh bay leaf

4 large shallots, chopped

2 carrots, chopped

150 g/5 oz. bacon lardons

250 ml/1 cup dry white wine

coarse sea salt and freshly ground black pepper

a roasting pan with a rack

Serves 4

Preheat the oven to 180°C (375°F) Gas 5.

Rub the guinea fowl all over with 1 tablespoon of the olive oil and season well, inside and out. Put on a rack set in a roasting pan and cook in the preheated oven for about 1 hour, until browned and the juices run clear when the thigh is pierced with a skewer.

Meanwhile, put the lentils, thyme and bay leaf into a saucepan and just cover with water. Bring to the boil, reduce the heat, cover with a lid and simmer gently for about 25 minutes, until tender. Drain and season with ½ teaspoon salt.

Heat the remaining 2 tablespoons oil in a frying pan/skillet. Add the shallots and carrots and cook for 3–5 minutes, until just tender. Stir in the bacon lardons and cook, stirring, until well browned. Add the wine and cook over high heat until reduced by half. Add the lentils, discard the herbs and set aside.

Remove the guinea fowl from the oven, cover and let stand for 10 minutes. Carve into serving pieces and serve immediately, with the lentils.

If you can find imported French duck magrets, they are worth buying, both for the flavour and for the size. If you use domestic duck breasts, cooking time will be less and you will probably need two per person. Serve with sautéed or roasted potatoes and a red wine such as Madiran.

Duck breasts with peppercorns

Magret de canard aux deux poivres

2 French duck magrets or 4 duck breasts, about 650 g/1½ lbs.

3 tablespoons Cognac

200 ml/1 cup crème fraîche or sour cream

1 tablespoon green peppercorns in brine, drained

1 tablespoon coarsely ground black pepper

coarse sea salt

Serves 2

Trim the excess fat from around the duck breasts, then score the skin in a diamond pattern.

Heat a heavy frying pan/skillet. When hot, add the duck skin-side first and cook for 7–8 minutes. Turn over the duck and cook the other side for 4–5 minutes, depending on thickness. Remove from the pan, season with salt and keep warm.

Drain almost all the fat from the pan. Return to the heat and add the Cognac, scraping the bottom of the pan. Stir in the crème fraîche or sour cream, green peppercorns and black pepper. Cook for 1 minute.

Slice the duck diagonally lengthways and put on serving plates. Pour the sauce over the top and serve immediately.

Rabbit with prunes

Lapin aux pruneaux

Rabbit and prunes don't really have a season, but this somehow seems autumnal, just the thing when the days are getting shorter and cooler, and it's nice to fill the house with appetizing aromas. A more apt name would be Drunken Rabbit, because there is so much wine, Cognac and port. But prunes it is, and they do play a vital part, adding a pleasant sweetness to the rich, velvety sauce and salty bacon lardons. Serve it with fresh pasta tossed in butter – tagliatelle is ideal. Chicken can be substituted for the rabbit, but don't cook it for as long.

1 rabbit, cut into 7–8 pieces
2 tablespoons sunflower oil
30 g/2 tablespoons unsalted butter
2 onions, halved and sliced
200 g/7 oz. bacon lardons
about 100 g/1 cup plain/all-purpose
  flour
125 ml/½ cup port
400 g/2½ cups plump prunes,
  preferably French
1 tablespoon crème fraîche or
  sour cream
coarse sea salt and freshly ground
  black pepper
tagliatelle, to serve

Marinade

1 onion, chopped
1 carrot, chopped
2 garlic cloves, crushed
2 sprigs of thyme
1 fresh bay leaf
750 ml/3¼ cups red wine
250 ml/1 cup Cognac
a few black or green peppercorns

a large flameproof casserole dish

Serves 4

One day before serving, mix all the marinade ingredients in a non-reactive bowl. Add the rabbit pieces, cover and refrigerate overnight.

When ready to cook, remove the rabbit from the marinade, strain the liquid and reserve. Discard all the vegetables but keep the thyme and bay leaf. Pat the rabbit pieces dry with kitchen paper/paper towels.

Heat 1 tablespoon of the oil and half the butter in a large flameproof casserole dish. Add the onions and bacon lardons and cook over high heat for 5 minutes, until brown. Remove from the casserole dish and set aside.

Put the flour on a plate and add the rabbit pieces, turning to coat lightly. Add the remaining oil and butter to the casserole dish and heat. When sizzling, put the rabbit pieces in the casserole dish and brown all over. Pour in the strained marinating liquid, bacon and onion mixture and port. Add the reserved thyme and bay leaf and season with salt and pepper. Bring to the boil, skim off the foam, then lower the heat, cover and simmer for 45 minutes. Season to taste.

Transfer the rabbit pieces to a plate, add the prunes, increase the heat and cook the sauce for 10–15 minutes more, until thickened. Stir in the crème fraîche or sour cream, return the rabbit to the casserole dish and heat just to warm through; do not boil. Serve immediately with tagliatelle.

Fish and seafood

Sole meunière

I am utterly addicted to this dish with its buttery-lemony sauce. Sole is a well-crafted fish, both meaty and delicate at the same time, and is very easy to eat, bone-wise. Do not make this for a crowd, because you should eat it straight away and two soles are about all that will fit into the average frying pan/skillet. But it is ideal for a tête-à-tête, weekday or otherwise, when you need something elegant and satisfying, in no time at all. Serve with a nice dry French white wine such as a Chablis.

2–3 tablespoons plain/all-purpose flour
2 fresh sole, about 150 g/10 oz. each, skinned and cleaned
2 tablespoons sunflower oil
40 g/4 tablespoons unsalted butter
fine sea salt
freshly squeezed juice of ½ a lemon
a handful of flat-leaf parsley, finely chopped
lemon slices, to serve

Serves 2

Put the flour on a large plate, add the fish, cover with flour on both sides and shake off the excess.

Heat the oil and all but 2 tablespoons of the butter over medium-high heat in a non-stick frying pan/skillet large enough to hold both fish side by side. When it sizzles, add the sole and cook for about 3 minutes. Turn them over and cook on the other side for 3 minutes. Sprinkle the first side with salt while the second side is cooking.

When the fish is cooked through, transfer to warmed serving plates and season the second side.

Return the frying pan/skillet to the heat, add the remaining butter and melt over high heat. When it begins to sizzle, lower the heat and add the lemon juice. Cook, scraping the pan for about 10 seconds; do not let the butter burn. Pour the sauce over the fish and sprinkle with parsley. Serve immediately, garnished with thin slices of lemon.

Roughly translated, the English version of this dish means 'roast from the sea'. A gigot is the leg, usually of lamb, but here it refers to the sturdy, meaty nature of monkfish. Most other fish would be overwhelmed by the robust flavours in this Provençal preparation. There is certainly nothing fishy about this, which makes it ideal for those who are less than enthusiastic about eating food from the sea. Good fishmongers will make sure the thin grey membrane that lies under the skin is removed; but if it isn't, insist that it is, all the way down the tail, because it's a difficult job to do at home.

Whole roast monkfish Gigot de mer

1 monkfish tail, about 600 g/
  1 lb. 5 oz.

about 12 thin slices smoked bacon,
  pancetta or prosciutto – enough
  to cover the fish

2 tablespoons olive oil

200 g/1½ cups mushrooms, sliced

2 large garlic cloves, crushed

250 ml/1 cup dry white wine

1 kg/2 lbs. tomatoes, skinned,
  deseeded and chopped

2 tablespoons crème fraîche
  or sour cream

a handful of basil leaves, chopped

coarse sea salt and freshly
  ground black pepper

a large baking dish

Serves 4

Preheat the oven to 220°C (425°F) Gas 7.

Put the bacon on a work surface with the slices slightly overlapping each other. Lay the monkfish on top, belly up. Wrap it in the bacon with the ends overlapping across the belly. Turn it over, cover and set aside.

Heat the oil in a large frying pan/skillet. Add the mushrooms and a pinch of salt and cook for 3–5 minutes, until browned. Stir in the garlic, then add the wine and cook over high heat for 1 minute. Stir in the tomatoes, salt lightly and simmer gently for 5 minutes.

Pour the tomato sauce into a baking dish just large enough to hold the fish. Place the fish on top and roast in the preheated oven for 15 minutes. Lower the temperature to 200°C (400°F) Gas 6 and roast for 30 minutes more. Remove from the oven and transfer the fish to a plate. Stir the crème fraîche or sour cream and basil into the tomato sauce. Put the monkfish back on top and serve.

Sea bass and fennel are virtually inseparable in Provençal cuisine. The market fish stalls of the south always have a plentiful supply of gleaming silvery bass, and fennel grows wild all over the countryside, so it's no wonder. Saffron and harissa, a spicy Moroccan chilli/chili paste, are not traditional, but recipes and ingredients from the former French colonies in North Africa are now found all over France, especially in the south. Serve with a Bandol rosé.

Braised sea bass and fennel with saffron and harissa Bar braisé au fenouil epicé

3 tablespoons olive oil

1 onion, thinly sliced

300 g/10 oz. fennel bulbs, quartered and thinly sliced

500 ml/2 cups fresh fish stock

a large pinch of saffron threads

600 g/21 oz. red potatoes, peeled and cut into large chunks

4 small fresh sea bass, cleaned, scaled and heads removed if preferred

1–2 teaspoons harissa paste

coarse sea salt and freshly ground black pepper

Serves 4

Heat the oil in a large frying pan/skillet with a lid. Add the onion and fennel and cook for about 10 minutes, until lightly golden brown. Season with a little salt. Add the fish stock and saffron and simmer gently for 15 minutes.

Meanwhile, put the potatoes in a large saucepan/pot with sufficient water to cover and boil for 15–20 minutes, until tender. Drain, coarsely crush with a fork and set aside.

Season the fish inside and out. Put it on top of the fennel, cover and simmer gently for 10–15 minutes, until the fish is cooked through.

Remove the fish from the pan, set on large serving plates and warm in a low oven. Add the crushed potatoes and harissa to the pan and continue cooking, covered, for about 5 minutes more, until warmed through. Taste and adjust the seasoning, then spoon onto the plates beside the fish and serve.

*VARIATION Replace the potatoes with couscous, but serve alongside the fish instead of mixing it in; stir the harissa into the fennel before serving.

Tuna stew with chillies and potatoes

Thon marmitako

A traditional dish from the Basque region, where tuna abounds and chillies/chiles are appreciated more than in other parts of France. This is quick to prepare and doesn't require long simmering, perfect when you want something hearty and full of flavour in about an hour.

80 ml/⅓ cup olive oil

2 onions, sliced

3 green (bell) peppers, halved, deseeded and sliced

3 red (bell) peppers, halved, deseeded and sliced

750 g/1½ lbs. red tuna steaks, cut into 5-cm/2-inch pieces

3 large, hot green chillies/chiles, deseeded and sliced

4 ripe tomatoes, skinned, deseeded and chopped

4 garlic cloves, crushed

1 kg/2 lbs. new potatoes, peeled and cut into wedges

750 ml/3¼ cups dry white wine

coarse sea salt and freshly ground black pepper

baguette, to serve

Serves 4

Heat the oil in a large heavy-based saucepan. Add the onions and (bell) peppers and cook over high heat for 3–5 minutes, until brown. Transfer to a bowl and season with salt and pepper.

Add the tuna and chillies/chiles to the pan and cook for 3–5 minutes, just to sear. Add the tomatoes, garlic and potatoes and salt to taste and stir carefully.

Return the onion mixture to the pan and pour in the wine. Add 250 ml/1 cup water. Bring to the boil and boil for 1 minute, then reduce the heat, cover and simmer gently for 30–35 minutes, until the potatoes are cooked through. Serve immediately with a crusty baguette.

Mussels with fennel, tomatoes, garlic and saffron Moules à la bouillabaisse

Large bowls of steaming hot mussels are enjoyed all over France. The classic recipe is à la marinière, with shallots and white wine. My combination of ingredients evolved because I could eat mussels every day, just steamed plain, but not everyone shares my enthusiasm for them served this way. If, however, they come cooked in a garlicky, saffron-scented sauce, reminiscent of summer holidays, then most people are happy.

2 tablespoons olive oil
1 small onion, chopped
½ fennel bulb, chopped
4 garlic cloves, crushed
250 ml/1 cup dry white wine
400-g/14-oz. can chopped
   tomatoes
a pinch of saffron threads
1 kg/2 lbs. fresh mussels
a handful of flat-leaf parsley
   leaves, chopped
coarse sea salt and freshly
   ground black pepper
baguette, to serve

Serves 4

Heat the oil in a large frying pan/skillet. Add the onion and fennel and cook for 3–5 minutes, until soft. Add the garlic, wine and tomatoes. Boil for 1 minute, then reduce the heat, add the saffron and a pinch of salt. Simmer gently for 15 minutes.

Clean and debeard the mussels, discarding any that do not close. (To prepare mussels, see note on page 33.) Increase the heat under the sauce and, when boiling, add the prepared mussels. Cover and cook for 2–3 minutes, until the mussels open. Discard any that do not open. Sprinkle with parsley and serve immediately with crusty baguette.

*VARIATION Frites are the classic accompaniments for mussels when served as a main course. See the recipe on page 44.

Le grand aïoli

Salt cod and snails are traditional ingredients in this Provençal dish, but salmon and prawns/shrimp are often easier to come by. Be sure to use very good oil; despite great quantities of garlic, the flavour base of the aïoli comes from the oil, so it is worth investing in something special. Serve for a crowd, with everything freshly cooked and warmish, or at room temperature. Wash it all down with a chilled white or rosé from Provence.

300 g/10 oz. small new potatoes

4 tablespoons olive oil

4 fresh salmon steaks

200 g/8 oz. unpeeled prawn/
  shrimp tails

100 g/5 oz. asparagus tips

1 fresh bay leaf

6 baby carrots, sliced lengthways

1 cauliflower, broken into florets

1 broccoli, broken into florets

200 g/8 oz. baby courgettes/
  zucchini, halved lengthways

6 eggs

200 g/8 oz. fine green beans

150 g/6 oz. cherry tomatoes

4 cooked beetroot/beets

coarse sea salt

Aïöli

2 egg yolks

about 400 ml/1⅔ cups extra virgin
  olive oil

6 large garlic cloves

fine sea salt

Serves 6

To make the aïöli, put the egg yolks in a small, deep bowl. Whisk/beat well, then gradually whisk/beat in the oil, adding it a little at a time and whisking/beating vigorously, until the mixture is as thick as mayonnaise. Stir in the garlic and season to taste. Cover and set aside.

Put the potatoes in a saucepan with sufficient salted water to cover, bring to the boil and cook for 10–15 minutes, until tender. Drain and set aside.

Meanwhile, heat 1 tablespoon of the oil in a non-stick frying pan/skillet, add the salmon steaks and cook for about 3 minutes on each side, until just cooked through. Season and set aside. Heat another 1 tablespoon of the oil in the same pan. Add the prawns/shrimp and cook for 3–5 minutes, until pink and firm. Season and set aside.

Bring a saucepan of salted water to the boil and cook the asparagus tips and beans for about 3 minutes, until just tender. Drain and set aside.

Bring another saucepan of water to the boil with the bay leaf. Add the carrots and cook for 3–4 minutes, until just tender. Remove with a slotted spoon and set aside. Return the water to the boil, add the cauliflower and cook for about 5 minutes, until just tender. Remove with a slotted spoon and set aside. Return the water to the boil, add the broccoli and cook for 3–4 minutes, until just tender. Set aside.

Rub the courgettes/zucchini all over with the remaining oil. Heat a ridged stove-top grill pan. When hot, add the courgette/zucchini slices and cook for about 4 minutes on each side. (Alternatively, cook in a non-stick frying pan/skillet.) Season and set aside.

Put the eggs in a saucepan with sufficient water to cover. Bring to the boil and cook for 6 minutes from boiling point. Cool under running water, peel and slice.

Arrange all of the ingredients on a single platter and serve with the aïöli.

Simple dishes

Ratatouille

I first learned to make ratatouille from a friend's mother in her kitchen in Aix-en-Provence. Her method involves adding each vegetable separately, in the order which best suits their cooking requirements. It does make a difference because I've rarely tasted a ratatouille as good. It is also important to season each vegetable 'layer' individually. Finally, I prefer my ratatouille vegetables to be distinct from each another, so cut the pieces medium-large, about 3–4 cm/ 1½ inches. Serve with crusty bread.

1 kg/2 lbs. aubergines/eggplant, cut into pieces

6–7 extra virgin olive oil (see method)

2 medium onions, coarsely chopped

2 red (bell) peppers, halved, deseeded and cut into pieces

2 yellow (bell) peppers, halved, deseeded and cut into pieces

1 green (bell) pepper, halved, deseeded and cut into pieces

6 small courgettes/zucchini, about 750 g/1½ lbs., halved lengthways and sliced

5 garlic cloves, crushed

6 tomatoes, halved, deseeded and chopped

leaves from a small bunch of basil, coarsely chopped, plus a few extra shredded, to serve

coarse sea salt

a large flameproof casserole dish

Serves 4—6

Put the aubergine/eggplant pieces in a microwave-proof bowl with 3 tablespoons water and microwave on HIGH for 6 minutes. Drain and set aside.

Heat 3 tablespoons of the oil in a large flameproof casserole dish. Add the onions and cook for 3–5 minutes, until soft. Salt lightly.

Add all the (bell) peppers and cook for 5–8 minutes more, stirring often. Turn up the heat to keep the sizzling sound going, but take care not to let it burn. Salt lightly.

Add 1 more tablespoon of the oil and the courgettes/zucchini. Mix well and cook for about 5 minutes more, stirring occasionally. Salt lightly.

Add 2 more tablespoons of the oil and the drained aubergines/eggplant. Cook, stirring often, for 5 minutes more. Salt lightly.

Add 4 of the crushed garlic cloves and cook for 1 minute. Add 1 more tablespoon of the oil if necessary, and the tomatoes and chopped basil and stir well. Salt lightly. Cook for 5 minutes, then cover, reduce the heat and simmer gently for 30 minutes, checking occasionally.

Remove from the heat. Stir in the remaining garlic clove and shredded basil just before serving. This is best served at room temperature, but it still tastes nice hot. The longer you let it stand, the richer it tastes.

This bistro classic is a much more sophisticated version of macaroni and cheese. It is ideal for serving with beef stews, as the gratin is even better when mixed with broth.

Macaroni gratin Gratin de macaroni

300 g/10 oz. macaroni

500 ml/2 cups milk

3 tablespoons crème fraîche
or sour cream

60 g/4 tablespoons unsalted butter

4 tablespoons/¼ cup plain/
all-purpose flour

200 g/1⅔ cups finely grated
Beaufort cheese*

coarse sea salt and freshly
ground black pepper

*a baking dish, 30 cm/12 inches
long, greased with butter*

Serves 6

Cook the macaroni according to the packet instructions. Drain, rinse well and return to the empty saucepan.

Heat the milk in a saucepan and stir in the crème fraîche or sour cream. Melt the butter in a separate saucepan set over medium-high heat. Stir in the flour and cook, stirring constantly, for 3 minutes. Pour in the milk mixture and stir constantly until the mixture thickens. Season with salt and pepper.

Preheat the grill/broiler. Stir the milk mixture into the macaroni and taste, adding more salt and pepper if necessary. Transfer to the prepared baking dish and sprinkle with the cheese. Cook under the preheated grill/broiler for 10–15 minutes, until bubbling and browned. Serve hot.

*NOTE Beaufort is an alpine cheese, similar to Gruyère, but with a slightly sweeter, more pronounced nutty flavour. It is becoming more widely available outside France, my local supermarket always has some, but if you cannot find it, Emmental, Cantal or any firm, Cheddar-like cheese will do. The taste will be entirely different, of course.

Though pumpkin is not usually associated with French cooking, it is in fact a very traditional ingredient. In the south of France, when it is in season, it is often served as a gratin. The conventional recipe is simply a purée with béchamel and a topping of crisp, browned breadcrumbs. This version has rice, which gives it a more interesting texture and makes it substantial enough to be a meal on its own, served with salad greens.

Pumpkin and rice gratin Gratin de courge et de riz

1.5 kg/3 lbs. pumpkin

3 tablespoons olive oil

100 g/½ cup long grain rice

a sprig of thyme

3 tablespoons fresh breadcrumbs

a small handful of flat-leaf parsley, finely chopped

3 tablespoons crème fraîche or sour cream

75 g/¾ cup finely grated Gruyère cheese

coarse sea salt and freshly ground black pepper

a large baking dish, greased with butter

Serves 6

Peel and deseed the pumpkin and cut it into small cubes. Put in a large saucepan/pot with 2 tablespoons of the oil, a pinch of salt and 250 ml/1 cup water. Cook over low heat for 20–30 minutes, stirring often, until soft and adding more water as necessary.

Meanwhile, put the rice and the remaining 1 tablespoon oil in a separate saucepan and cook over medium heat, stirring to coat the grains. Add 250 ml/ 1 cup water, the thyme and a pinch of salt and bring to the boil. Cover and simmer for 10 minutes, until almost tender. Drain and discard the thyme.

Preheat the oven to 200°C (400°F) Gas 6. Mix the breadcrumbs with the parsley and a pinch of salt. Set aside.

Mash the cooked pumpkin into a coarse purée with a wooden spoon and stir in the cooked rice and crème fraîche or sour cream. Taste; the topping and cheese will add flavour, but the pumpkin mixture should be seasoned as well.

Spoon the pumpkin mixture into the prepared baking dish, spreading evenly. Sprinkle the cheese over the top, then follow with the breadcrumbs. Bake in the preheated oven for 20–30 minutes, until browned. Serve hot.

Aubergine, onion and tomato tian

Tian d'aubergines aux oignons et tomates

Tian is the Provençal name for a square earthenware baking dish, but I use a non-stick roasting pan and the tian still tastes great. Ideally, it should be served tepid or at room temperature, as it would be for the sweltering heat of a Provençal summer. The tian will improve with age and can easily be made one day in advance.

4 medium aubergines/eggplant, sliced crossways into 2 cm/ 1-inch pieces

5 tablespoons fresh breadcrumbs

½ teaspoon dried herbes de provence

about 125 ml/½ cup olive oil

2 large onions, sliced into thick rings

3 large tomatoes, sliced

40 g/¼ cup stoned/pitted black olives, sliced

coarse sea salt and freshly ground black pepper

Tomato sauce

1 tablespoon olive oil

3 garlic cloves

1.5 kg/3 lbs. tomatoes, skinned, deseeded and chopped

a pinch of sugar

a small handful of basil, chopped

a small handful of flat-leaf parsley, chopped

coarse sea salt and freshly ground black pepper

a non-stick roasting pan or rectangular baking dish

Serves 4—6

Preheat the oven to 200°C (400°F) Gas 6.

To make the tomato sauce, heat the oil in a saucepan, add the garlic and cook for 1–2 minutes, until just soft. Add the tomatoes, sugar and salt to taste. Cover and simmer gently for 10 minutes. Stir in the basil and parsley and set aside.

Bring a large saucepan/pot of water to the boil and add a pinch of salt. Add the aubergine/eggplant slices and cook for 3–5 minutes, until just blanched and tender. Drain well.

Put the breadcrumbs, dried herbs and a pinch of salt in a bowl, mix well and set aside.

Pour 3–4 tablespoons of the oil into the baking dish, arrange the aubergine/ eggplant rounds on top and drizzle with some of the remaining oil. Top with the onion rings and sprinkle with salt and pepper. Dot the tomato sauce on top, spreading as evenly as possible. Arrange the tomato slices on top, sprinkle with the breadcrumbs, followed by the olives. Bake in the preheated oven for about 45 minutes, until well browned. Serve hot or warm.

Potatoes with reblochon Tartiflette

A meal in itself, this is very rich and filling, just the sort of thing to serve after a day on the ski slopes. You might find this on menus in the Savoie region of France, though it is not, strictly speaking, a traditional recipe. It was 'invented' in the 1980s by the local cheese committee to help sell more Reblochon cheese – and I'm sold! Serve with mixed salad greens and a bottle of chilled vin d'Aprémont from the Savoie, which is what you should use in the cooking.

1 kg/2¼ lbs. waxy salad-style potatoes
1 fresh bay leaf
60 g/4 tablespoons unsalted butter
2 onions, halved and sliced
150 g/5 oz. bacon lardons
75 ml/⅓ cup dry white wine
500-g/1-lb. Reblochon cheese*
coarse sea salt and freshly ground black pepper

a baking dish, about 30 cm/ 12 inches long, greased with butter

Serves 6

Put the potatoes in a large saucepan/pot, then add the bay leaf and sufficient cold water to cover. Bring to the boil, add a generous pinch of salt and cook for about 15 minutes, until the potatoes are just tender. Drain. When cool enough to handle, peel and slice.

Melt half the butter in a frying pan/skillet, add the onions and bacon lardons and cook until just browned. Remove with a slotted spoon and set aside. Add the remaining butter to the pan with the potatoes and cook gently for 5 minutes. Stir carefully without breaking too many potato slices. Add the wine, bring to the boil and boil for 1 minute. Season with salt and pepper.

Preheat the oven to 220°C (425°F) Gas 7. Arrange the potatoes in the prepared baking dish. Spoon the onions and bacon on top of the potatoes. Scrub the rind of the cheese lightly with a vegetable brush, then cut into 8 wedges. Cut each piece in half through the middle, so each has skin on one side only. Put the cheese on top of the potatoes, skin-side up. Cover with foil and bake in the preheated oven for 15 minutes. Remove the foil and bake for 15–20 minutes more, until browned. Serve hot.

*NOTE If Reblochon is unavailable, substitute any other French mountain cheese, such as Emmental, Cantal or a Pyrénées. A firm goats' cheese such as Crottin de Chavignol, is also very nice. Alternatively, this recipe is a great way to clear out a cluttered cheese compartment, especially the post-dinner party syndrome of lovely but unfinished cheeses. Simply crumble or slice whatever you've got and arrange it on top of the potatoes before baking.

Salads and sides

Mixed leaf salad with garlic vinaigrette

Salade verte, vinaigrette à l'ail

*Green salads do not appear as often on French menus as a appetizer or side dish
as they do in other countries, though they are still served in very traditional bistros.
Home is the main place for eating salads, and they're eaten daily, usually after the
main course and either before or with the cheese. Raw garlic is not always included,
but the vinaigrette method is classic, the way I was taught to make it when I first
moved to France, and the way I've made it ever since.*

2 tablespoons wine vinegar
½ teaspoon fine sea salt
1 teaspoon Dijon mustard
6 tablespoons olive oil
2 garlic cloves, crushed
freshly ground white pepper
250 g/8 oz. tender, mixed salad
  leaves, washed and dried
a handful of flat-leaf parsley,
  coarsely chopped
a small bunch of chives, snipped

Serves 4

Put the vinegar in a salad bowl. Using a fork or a small whisk, stir in the salt
until almost dissolved. You may have to tilt the bowl so the vinegar is deep
enough to have something to stir around.

Stir in the mustard until completely blended. Add the oil, a tablespoon at
a time, whisking/beating well between each addition, until emulsified. Mix
in the garlic and add pepper to taste.

If you like a powerful garlic punch, add the salad leaves to the bowl with
the parsley and chives, then toss and serve immediately. I prefer to let the
garlic sit in the dressing for at least 30 minutes to mellow it a bit. In any
case, do not add the salad leaves until you are ready to serve or they will
become soggy.

Tomato salad with anchovy vinaigrette

Salade de tomates, vinaigrette à l'anchoïade

Anchoïade is a Provençal anchovy paste, which is spread thickly on grilled/broiled bread slices or served with raw vegetables as an appetizer. Here it becomes a dressing for hopefully very ripe, flavourful tomatoes. If these are not available, use boiled baby new potatoes instead and toss while the potatoes are still warm. Serve with a chilled Provençal rosé and lots of crusty bread.

750 g/1½ lbs. ripe vine tomatoes
1 large shallot, or 1 small red onion, thinly sliced
coarse sea salt and freshly ground black pepper

Anchovy vinaigrette

1 garlic clove
½ teaspoon Dijon mustard
2 tablespoons white wine vinegar
6 anchovy fillets, packed in oil
8 tablespoons extra virgin olive oil
a small handful of basil leaves
a handful of flat-leaf parsley, finely chopped
freshly ground black pepper
crusty bread, to serve

Serves 4

To make the vinaigrette, put the garlic, mustard, vinegar and anchovies in a small food processor and blend well. Add the oil, 1 tablespoon at a time, then blend in the basil, reserving a few leaves. Season with pepper and set aside.

Cut the tomatoes into quarters or eighths, depending on their size. Arrange on a plate and sprinkle with the sliced shallot. Season lightly with salt, then spoon the dressing over the top. Sprinkle with the parsley, reserved basil leaves and freshly ground black pepper. Serve at room temperature with crusty bread.

Mine is a family of serial salad eaters, but I'd never heard of chicory/endive until moving to France. In those days, it was still a fairly bitter thing, available only in winter and an acquired taste, but it has come a long way. Developed unintentionally by a gardener at the Brussels botanical gardens in the middle of the nineteenth century, chicory/endive is now cultivated for a good part of the year, and modern varieties have none of the bitterness of their ancestors. When buying, choose a very pale variety with only a hint of green; they grow in the dark, so colour on the leaves is a sign that they have been exposed to the light and are not as fresh. Also, big is not necessarily better.*

Chicory salad with roquefort, celery and walnuts
Salade d'endives aux roquefort, céleri et noix

4–5 heads of chicory/Belgian endive, about 600 g/1¼ lbs., halved, cored and thinly sliced

2 celery sticks/stalks, thinly sliced, plus a few leaves, torn

75 g/3 oz. Roquefort cheese, crumbled

50 g/⅓ cup shelled walnuts, chopped

a handful of flat-leaf parsley, finely chopped

crusty bread, to serve

Walnut vinaigrette

2 tablespoons wine vinegar

1 teaspoon fine sea salt

1 teaspoon Dijon mustard

7 tablespoons sunflower oil (see method)

1 tablespoon walnut oil (optional)

freshly ground white pepper

Serves 4

To prepare the vinaigrette, put the vinegar in a salad bowl. Using a fork or a small whisk, stir in the salt until almost dissolved. You may have to tilt the bowl so the vinegar is deep enough to have something to stir.

Mix in the mustard until completely blended. Add the oil, a tablespoon at a time, beating well between each addition, until emulsified. If you're using the walnut oil, use one less tablespoon of sunflower oil. Add pepper to taste.

Just before you're ready to serve the salad, add the chicory/endive, celery, Roquefort, walnuts and parsley and toss well. Serve immediately, with plenty of crusty bread.

Lovely leeks are delicious with this lively herb-studded sauce. Serve at the start of a substantial spread, to allow room for expansion, or as part of a light lunch with the Goats' Cheese Tart on page 19. If you can't find sorrel, it will be a shame, but the recipe works without, so don't feel obliged to replace it with anything.

Baby leeks with herb vinaigrette

Poireaux, vinaigrette aux herbes

750 g/1½ lbs baby leeks
60 ml/¼ cup wine vinegar
1 teaspoon Dijon mustard
1 teaspoon fine sea salt
250 ml/1 cup sunflower oil
a small handful of flat-leaf parsley
a small handful of watercress
a small handful of tarragon
3 sorrel leaves
2 shallots, thinly sliced
a small bunch of chives, snipped
freshly ground black pepper

Serves 4

Put the leeks in the top of a steamer and cook for about 7–10 minutes, until tender. Remove and set aside to drain.

To make the vinaigrette, put the vinegar, mustard and salt in a small food processor and blend well. Add about 75 ml/⅓ cup of the oil and blend for a few seconds. Continue adding the oil, a little at a time, and blending until the vinaigrette is emulsified. Add the parsley, watercress, tarragon and sorrel and pulse again to chop. Add pepper to taste. (Alternatively, see page 101 for the hand-mixing method, and you'll have to chop all the herbs finely.)

If the leeks are still too wet, pat dry with kitchen paper/paper towels. Arrange the leeks in a serving dish, spoon the vinaigrette over the top and sprinkle with shallot slices and chives. Serve with any remaining vinaigrette on the side.

Poor old celery; it is more often an ingredient than the star of a dish. However, in this traditional Provençal recipe, it takes centre stage. Beef is the ideal complement to the trinity of celery, tomatoes and anchovies, so serve this with roast beef or steaks.

Braised celery Céleri braisé

2 whole bunches of celery
2 tablespoons olive oil
75 g/3 oz. bacon lardons
1 onion, halved, then quartered and sliced
1 carrot, halved lengthways, then quartered and sliced
2 garlic cloves, sliced
200 g/1 cup canned chopped tomatoes
250 ml/1 cup dry white wine
1 fresh bay leaf
8 canned anchovy fillets, chopped
a handful of flat-leaf parsley, chopped
coarse sea salt and freshly ground black pepper

Serves 4–6

Remove any tough outer sticks from the celery and trim the tips so they will just fit into a large frying pan/skillet with a lid.

Bring a large saucepan/pot of water to the boil. Add a pinch of salt, then the celery and simmer gently for 10 minutes to blanch. Remove, drain and pat dry with kitchen paper/paper towels.

Heat the oil in the frying pan/skillet. Add the bacon lardons, onion and carrot and cook gently until lightly browned. Add the celery and a little salt and pepper and cook just to brown, then remove.

Add the garlic, cook for 1 minute, then add the tomatoes, wine and bay leaf. Bring to the boil and cook for 1 minute. Add the celery, cover and simmer gently for 30 minutes, turning the celery once during cooking.

Transfer the celery to a serving dish. Increase the heat and cook the sauce for about 10 minutes, to reduce it slightly. Pour it over the celery, sprinkle with the anchovies and parsley and serve.

Carrots with cream and herbs

Carottes à la crème aux herbes

Thyme is omnipresent in French cuisine. Here, it transforms what would otherwise be ordinary boiled carrots into something subtly sumptuous. The crème fraîche or sour cream helps too. You can substitute steamed baby leeks for the carrots, but stir in a tablespoon or so of butter when adding the crème fraîche.

800 g/2 lbs. mini carrots, trimmed,
   or medium carrots
50 g/3 tablespoons unsalted butter
a sprig of thyme
2 tablespoons crème fraîche or sour cream
several sprigs of chervil, snipped
a small bunch of chives, snipped
fine sea salt

Serves 4

If using larger carrots, cut them diagonally into 5-cm/2-inch slices. Put in a large saucepan/pot (the carrots should fit in a single layer to ensure even cooking). Add the butter and set over low heat. Cook for 3 minutes, until the butter has melted and coated the carrots. Half fill the saucepan with water, then add a pinch of salt and the thyme. Cover and cook for 10–20 minutes, until the water is almost completely evaporated.

Stir in the crème fraîche or sour cream and add salt to taste. Sprinkle the chervil and chives over the top, mix well and serve.

French beans with garlic

Haricots verts à l'ail

French beans are a classic accompaniment for lamb, but they are equally nice with fish and chicken. You can also serve at room temperature, as part of a salad buffet. Instead of the cooked beans, try long, thin slices of steamed courgettes/zucchini, sautéed with the garlic.

625 g/1½ lbs. fine green beans, trimmed
2 tablespoons olive oil
1 tablespoon unsalted butter
2 garlic cloves, crushed
a handful of flat-leaf parsley, chopped
1 teaspoon freshly squeezed lemon juice
sea salt and freshly ground black pepper

Serves 4

Bring a large saucepan/pot of water to the boil. Add the beans and cook for 3–4 minutes from the time the water returns to the boil. Drain and refresh under cold running water. Set aside.

Heat the oil and butter in a frying pan/skillet. Add the garlic, beans and salt, and cook on high heat for 1 minute, stirring. Remove from the heat and stir in the parsley and lemon juice. Sprinkle with pepper and serve.

Spinach flan Flan d'épinards

Years ago, I went on a wine-buying mission with some friends in the Jura region of France. We stopped for lunch at a small hotel, but it was very late in the day, so we had to take what we were given. The offering was roast pork, served with a glorious mixture of vegetables, all thinly sliced and baked in a fabulous savoury custard. Back home, I tried a similar dish using just spinach, because that's what was on hand, and it proved a great success.

500 g/1 lb. fresh spinach

3–5 tablespoons olive oil

200 ml/¾ cup crème fraîche
  or sour cream

2 eggs

1 teaspoon coarse sea salt

a pinch of freshly grated nutmeg

1 tablespoon unsalted butter

a baking dish, 30 cm/12 inches long

Serves 4

Preheat the oven to 180°C (350°F) Gas 4.

Wash the spinach, then spin-dry in a salad spinner. Working in batches, heat 1 tablespoon of the oil in a non-stick frying pan/skillet and add a mound of spinach. Cook the spinach over high heat, stirring until all the leaves have just wilted. Transfer to a plastic colander and let drain. Continue cooking until all the spinach has been wilted.

Chop the spinach coarsely. Put the crème fraîche or sour cream, eggs, salt and nutmeg in a bowl and whisk/beat well. Stir in the spinach.

Spread the butter in the bottom of a baking dish. Transfer the spinach mixture to the dish and bake in the preheated oven for 25–30 minutes, until just set. Serve hot.

Peas, asparagus and baby lettuce

Petits pois, asperges et laitues à la française

Freshly shelled peas with lettuce form one of the classics of French cuisine. Teamed with asparagus in a light buttery sauce, they're ideal for serving with roast poultry or grilled/broiled fish. Bacon makes a nice addition so stir in about 75 g/¼ cup fried bacon lardons, just before serving, if liked.

75 g/6 tablespoons unsalted butter
3–4 shallots, sliced into rounds
3 Little Gem/Bibb lettuces, quartered
100 g/4 oz. asparagus tips, halved
400 g/2 cups shelled fresh peas
coarse sea salt
sprigs of chervil or flat-leaf parsley, finely chopped, or chives, snipped, to serve

Serves 4

Melt half the butter in a saucepan with a lid. Add the shallots and lettuce and cover. Cook, stirring often, for 8–10 minutes, until tender. Season with salt, add the remaining butter and the asparagus, cover and cook for 5 minutes more. Add the peas, cover and cook for 3 minutes more. Taste for seasoning, sprinkle with the herbs and serve.

*VARIATION For a more substantial side dish, or even a light meal, add 300 g/10 oz. sliced baby carrots and a splash of water when cooking the lettuce. Before serving, gently stir in more butter or 1 tablespoon crème fraîche or sour cream and add 500 g/1 lb. boiled small new potatoes, sliced into wedges.

This recipe goes especially well with roast pork. The secret of delicious cauliflower is to blanch it first; if you parboil it with a bay leaf, the unpleasant cabbage aroma disappears completely.

Cauliflower gratin Gratin de chou-fleur

1 large cauliflower, separated
    into large florets

1 fresh bay leaf

500 ml/2 cups double/heavy cream

1 egg

2 teaspoons Dijon mustard

160 g/1½ cups grated Comté
    cheese

coarse sea salt

*a baking dish, about 25 cm/
    10 inches diameter, greased
    with butter*

Serves 4—6

Bring a large saucepan/pot of water to the boil, add the bay leaf, salt generously, then add the cauliflower florets. Cook for about 10 minutes, until still slightly firm. Drain and set aside.

Put the cream in a saucepan and bring to the boil. Boil for 10 minutes. Add a spoonful of hot milk to the beaten egg to warm it, then stir the egg, mustard and 1 teaspoon salt into the cream.

Preheat the oven to 200°C (400°F) Gas 6. Divide the cauliflower into smaller florets, then stir them into the cream sauce. Transfer to the prepared baking dish and sprinkle the cheese over the top in an even layer.

Bake in the preheated oven for 40–45 minutes, until golden. Serve hot.

*NOTE Like Gruyère, Comté is a mountain cheese – from the Franche-Comté region to be precise – but the similarity stops there. Comté's distinct flavour comes from the milk used in the making, so the flavour varies with the seasons. A springtime diet of tender young shoots delivers milk that is very different from its winter counterpart, nourished mainly on hay. I've never met a Comté I didn't like, but it is darker in colour and fruitier in summer, paler and more nutty in winter. Use Emmental or Cantal if it is unavailable.

Braised red cabbage with chestnuts and apples
Chou rouge aux marrons et aux pommes

There are several regional variations on this recipe and it was difficult to choose which one to include. Chou rouge à la flammande has apples, à la limousine has chestnuts. This recipe has it all, with some Alsatian Riesling and bacon as well – serve it with grilled/broiled sausages, pork chops or roasts, and the same wine as used in the cooking. It is also fantastic with Christmas goose.

1 red cabbage

3 tablespoons unsalted butter

1 onion, halved and thinly sliced

75 g/3 oz. bacon lardons

3 cooking apples, peeled, cored and chopped

200 g/7 oz. vacuum-packed whole peeled chestnuts

2 teaspoons coarse sea salt

250 ml/1 cup dry white wine, preferably Riesling

1 tablespoon sugar

Serves 4—6

Cut the cabbage in quarters, then core and slice thinly.

Melt 2 tablespoons of the butter in a frying pan/skillet. Add the onion and lardons and cook for about 3 minutes, until soft.

Add the remaining butter, the cabbage, apples and chestnuts and stir well. Season with salt, then add the wine, sugar and 250 ml/1 cup water.

Bring to the boil, boil for 1 minute, then cover and simmer gently for about 45 minutes, until the cabbage is tender.

Creamy potato gratin

Gratin dauphinois

Cream and potatoes, mingling in the heat of the oven, are almost all you'll find in this well-loved dish. If it had cheese, it wouldn't be a true dauphinois. Serve on its own, with a mixed green salad, or as a partner for simple roast meat or poultry.

2 kg/4½ lbs. waxy salad-style potatoes, cut in half if large

2 litres/quarts whole milk

1 fresh bay leaf

30 g/2 tablespoons unsalted butter

500 ml/2 cups whipping cream

a pinch of grated nutmeg

coarse sea salt

a baking dish, 30 cm/12 inches long

Serves 4–6

Preheat the oven to 180°C (350°F) Gas 4.

Put the potatoes in a large saucepan/pot with the milk and bay leaf. Bring to the boil, then reduce the heat, add a pinch of salt and simmer gently for 5–10 minutes, until part-cooked. Drain and when cool enough to handle (but still hot), slice into rounds about 3 mm/⅛ inch thick.

Spread the butter in the bottom of the baking dish. Arrange half the potato slices in the dish and sprinkle with salt. Put the remaining potato slices on top and sprinkle with more salt. Pour in the cream and sprinkle with the nutmeg.

Bake in the preheated oven for 45 minutes, until golden and the cream is almost absorbed, but not completely. Serve hot.

Sweet things

Sugared strawberries   Fraises au sucre

As soon as it's strawberry season, you'll find this on menus all over France, though Plougastel in Brittany claims to be home to the best of the French strawberry crop. Wherever they come from, lemon juice is key, enhancing the flavour of the fruit as well as adding tartness to show off the sugar.

1 kg/2 lbs. strawberries,
 at room temperature

freshly squeezed juice of 1 lemon

3–5 tablespoons caster/superfine
 sugar

crème fraîche, sour cream or
 whipped cream, to serve

Serves 4—6

Trim the strawberries and put them in a pretty bowl. Add the lemon juice and 3 tablespoons of the sugar. Mix gently but thoroughly and let stand for about 15 minutes. Taste, and add more sugar if necessary.

This dish improves with standing, but don't leave it too long. If you make it just before you're ready to begin your meal, it will be ready in time for dessert.

If using crème fraîche, sweeten it with a spoonful of caster/superfine sugar.

*Variation Peach or nectarine slices can be substituted for the strawberries, if you like to stick to single fruit, or use a mixture of soft fruit including redcurrants, blueberries, raspberries and blackberries.

Raspberry cream   Crème aux framboises

I once stayed with a family in the Provençal village of Crest, where I remember having something similar made with fraise des bois (wild strawberries) and then again, with another family in Alsace, made with blueberries we had spent the afternoon gathering. But I also came across a recipe in an Elizabeth David book, which is what reminded me of its existence.

350 g/12 oz. raspberries, fresh or frozen and thawed plus 1 small punnet/basket of fresh raspberries

5–6 tablespoons caster/superfine sugar, to taste

250 ml/1 cup whipping cream, chilled

1 large egg white

sprigs of mint, to serve

Serves 4

Put the raspberries in a blender or food processor and blend until smooth. Press through a sieve/strainer to obtain a smooth purée; you should have about 200 ml/ 1 cup. Stir in 4–5 tablespoons of the sugar. Set aside.

Put the cream in a large bowl and whisk/beat with an electric mixer until it holds firm peaks. Set aside.

Whisk/beat the egg white with 1 tablespoon of the sugar until it holds firm peaks. Fold the beaten egg white and raspberry purée into the cream.

Divide the mixture between 4 serving glasses, filling half-way. Set aside 4 fresh raspberries, then divide the remaining fresh ones between the glasses and top with the remaining raspberry cream.

Decorate the top of each with a fresh raspberry and a mint sprig. Chill for up to 6 hours. Serve cold.

*VARIATION Use fromage frais in place of the whipped cream, or use half whipped cream and half fromage frais. This can also be made with strawberries or mixed berries, though you will have to adjust the sugar content. Sweeten the fruit purée gradually, tasting as you go, until it isto your liking.

You don't need any special equipment to make a really fantastic frozen dessert, as this recipe will prove. It is also easy, fast and probably takes first place ahead of all the other recipes in this book. Hard to believe, but this is better than chocolate cake. You can also freeze it in individual silicone moulds, but be sure to choose a shape that will allow for a meringue in the middle of each one.

Honey parfait with meringue and caramelized pistachios Parfait meringué au miel et aux pistaches caramelisées

100 g/1 cup shelled pistachio nuts

50 g/¼ cup sugar

300 ml/1¼ cups whipping cream, chilled

2 large eggs, separated

100 g/scant ⅓ cup clear honey

8–10 mini meringues or 6–8 meringue nests

a loaf pan or other freezer-proof mould

Serves 6

Put the pistachios and sugar in a non-stick saucepan. Cook over medium/high heat, stirring, until they begin to caramelize. Remove from the pan and let cool. Grind coarsely in a food processor or by putting between 2 sheets of baking parchment and crushing with a rolling pin.

Put the cream in a large bowl and whisk/beat until firm. Set aside. Put the egg yolks and honey in a second bowl, whisk/beat well, then set aside. Put the egg whites in a third bowl and beat until they hold stiff peaks. Set aside.

Fold the egg yolk mixture into the cream until blended. Gently fold in the egg whites until just blended. Fold in the pistachios.

Spoon half the mixture into a freezer-proof mould. Arrange the meringues on top in a single layer – nests may have to be broken up slightly depending on size, but not too small, because you want big pieces of meringue in the finished dish. Cover with the remaining parfait mixture and smooth the top. Cover with clingfilm/plastic wrap and freeze for about 6–8 hours or overnight, until firm. Scoop into tall glasses to serve.

Poached peaches in vanilla syrup

Les pêches pochées au sirop vanillé

Poached peaches are a very simple and elegant way to end a heavy meal. To jazz it up a bit, serve the peaches with a fresh raspberry coulis and vanilla ice cream and, voilà, Peach Melba, the famous dessert created by Escoffier for the great soprano, Dame Nellie Melba.

100 g/½ cup caster/superfine sugar
1 vanilla pod/bean, split lengthways with a small sharp knife
6 peaches, ripe but not too soft
sweetened crème fraîche or whipped cream, to serve

Serves 6

Put 1.5 litres/6 cups water into a saucepan. Add the sugar and vanilla pod/bean, bring just to the boil, then simmer gently.

Bring another saucepan of water to the boil. Make a criss-cross incision in the base of each peach and plunge it into the boiling water for 30 seconds. Remove with a slotted spoon. Using a small knife, peel off the skin. Transfer the peeled peaches to the sugar syrup as they are peeled. Cover with a round of baking parchment and poach for 15–25 minutes, until tender.

Remove from the syrup with a slotted spoon. Increase the heat under the saucepan and boil the syrup to reduce by half. Let cool.

Serve in small bowls, with some of the poaching liquid and a dollop of the cream of your choice.

Poached pears in honey wine

Les poires pochées au vin et au miel

This is a classic recipe but you can also poach the pears in the same way as the peaches (left) and serve with a chocolate sauce and vanilla ice cream – also known as Poires Belle Hélène.

750 ml/3¼ cups fruity red wine
4 tablespoons clear honey
a pinch of ground cinnamon
6 pears, ripe but not too soft

Serves 6

Put the wine, honey and cinnamon in a saucepan large enough to take all the pears in one layer, stems upward. (Don't add the pears yet.) Bring just to the boil, then simmer gently.

Using a vegetable peeler, peel the fruit, leaving the stems intact. Put into the poaching liquid, stems upward. Poach for 15–25 minutes, until tender. Remove from the syrup with a slotted spoon. Increase the heat and boil the liquid to reduce by half. Let cool. Serve in small bowls, with some of the honey wine spooned over the top.

Chocolate mousse Mousse au chocolat

This is very easy to make and ideal for entertaining, since it should be made one day in advance. It is also deceptively rich, thanks to the egg yolks, which can be reduced in quantity or omitted altogether. It is important to use good-quality chocolate, but anything over 70 per cent cocoa solids will be too much. In traditional bistros, chocolate mousse is often served in a single, large bowl and passed around the table for diners to help themselves, so if you're expecting a crowd, double the recipe and do the same.

200 g/7 oz. dark chocolate, broken into pieces

30 g/2 tablespoons unsalted butter, cut into small pieces

1 vanilla pod/bean, split lengthways with a small sharp knife

3 eggs, separated

a pinch of salt

2 tablespoons caster/superfine sugar

sweetened crème fraîche, sour cream or whipped cream, to serve (optional)

Serves 4

Put the chocolate in a glass bowl and melt in the microwave on HIGH for 40 seconds. Remove, stir and repeat until almost completely melted. Remove, then stir in the butter. Using the tip of a small knife, scrape the black seeds from the vanilla pod/bean and put into the chocolate. Add the egg yolks, stir and set aside.

Using an electric mixer, whisk/beat the egg whites and salt until foaming. Continue whisking/beating and add the sugar. Whisk/beat on high until glossy and firm.

Carefully fold the whites into the chocolate with a rubber spatula until no more white specks can be seen.

Transfer the mousse to serving dishes and refrigerate for at least 6 hours, but overnight is best.

*NOTE If you don't have a microwave, put the chocolate in a bowl over a saucepan of simmering water – don't let the water touch the bottom of the bowl. Leave until melted, stirring occasionally.

Caramel custard Crème renversée au caramel

These are neither too sweet, nor too heavy; the perfect ending to a substantial meal. Preparation is simple but there are a few tricks to facilitate unmoulding. First, don't use moulds that are too deep (and don't overfill them). Then, let the custards stand in the bain-marie for a good 15 minutes before removing them to cool completely. According to a reliable old French cookbook of mine, this allows the custard to settle and solidify, making it easier to turn out. Just before serving, run a knife around the inside edge, hold an upturned plate over the top and flip over to release the custard.

750 ml/3 cups whole milk

1 vanilla pod/bean, split lengthways with a small sharp knife

180 g/¾ cup plus 2 tablespoons sugar

5 eggs

a pinch of salt

8 ramekin dishes

a roasting pan, large enough to hold the ramekins

Serves 8

Put the milk, vanilla pod/bean and its seeds in a saucepan and bring to the boil over medium heat. Immediately remove from the heat, cover and let stand while you make the caramel.

For the caramel, put 100 g/½ cup of the sugar, the salt and 4 tablespoons water in a small heavy-based saucepan, preferably with a pouring lip. Heat until the sugar turns a deep caramel colour, then remove from the heat. When it stops sizzling, pour carefully into the ramekins. Take care not to let the caramel come into contact with your skin; it is very hot. Set the ramekins in a roasting pan and add enough boiling water to come half-way up the sides – this is called a bain-marie. Set aside.

Add the remaining sugar and the salt to the saucepan of warm milk and stir until dissolved. Remove the vanilla pod/bean.

Crack the eggs into another bowl and whisk/beat until smooth. Pour the warm milk into the eggs and stir well. Ladle into the ramekins.

Preheat the oven to 180°C (350°F) Gas 4. Carefully transfer the bain-marie with the ramekins into the preheated oven and bake for about 20–25 minutes, until the custard is set and a knife inserted into the middle comes out clean. Serve at room temperature either in their ramekins or inverted onto a plate so the caramel forms a pool of sweet sauce.

This very old-fashioned recipe evokes cries of 'oo-la, les petits pots ...' from French acquaintances of a certain age. It's the sort of thing an auntie would have made in the kitchen of her country house during the summer hols. And most respectable aunties would have had special little pots, about the size of espresso cups, solely for this purpose. You can also use regular crème brûlée ramekins. Good-quality chocolate is imperative for a good result.

Chocolate cream pots Petits pots au chocolat

250 ml/1 cup whole milk

250 ml/1 cup double/heavy cream

100 g/3½ oz. dark chocolate, with at least 70 per cent cocoa solids, finely chopped

3 large whole eggs plus 2 egg yolks

125 g/⅔ cup caster/superfine sugar

6 heatproof ramekins or similar

a baking dish, large enough to hold the ramekins

Makes 6

Put the milk and cream in a saucepan. Bring just to the boil and remove from the heat. Stir in the chocolate until melted.

Put the eggs, yolks and sugar in a large bowl and mix well, but don't whisk/beat until frothy; the finished dish should be smooth on top and whisking/beating too much will make too many bubbles that mar the surface. Pour in the milk mixture and stir gently until just mixed.

Bring a kettle of water to the boil and preheat the oven to 180°C (350°F) Gas 4.

Set the ramekins in a baking dish. Ladle the chocolate mixture into each ramekin to fill well. Open the preheated oven, pull out the shelf and set the baking dish with the ramekins on the shelf. Pour the boiling water into the dish to come about two-thirds up the sides of the ramekins. Cover the entire dish tightly with aluminium foil. Carefully push the shelf back in.

Cook for 20–25 minutes, until just set and still a bit jiggly in the middle. Remove the dish from the oven, let stand for 5 minutes, then remove the ramekins from the water bath. Let cool uncovered and serve warm or at room temperature.

The sweet and frothy egg mixture spread on top of the fruit is called a sabayon, making this a very easy and elegant dessert. It is best when made with a bit of something alcoholic – I prefer Muscat de Beaumes de Venise. The recipe requires only a small amount of wine and the remainder is just the thing to drink with this dish – ideal for special occasions.

Berry gratin De fruits des bois

600 g/1¼ lbs. frozen mixed berries, thawed

5 large egg yolks and 3 egg whites

80 g/⅓ cup caster/superfine sugar

1 tablespoon clear honey

125 ml/½ cup sweet dessert wine or Champagne (optional)

1–2 tablespoons icing/confectioners' sugar

4 shallow, ovenproof gratin dishes

Serves 4

Divide the fruit between the gratin dishes. Preheat the grill/broiler to high.

Bring a saucepan of water just to simmering point. Choose a heatproof bowl (glass is ideal) that will sit tightly on top of the saucepan. Put the egg yolks and caster/superfine sugar in the bowl and whisk/beat, off the heat, until blended. Transfer the bowl to the saucepan and continue whisking/beating (over the heat) for 2–4 minutes, until the mixture is thick and frothy. Don't let the water boil. Whisk/beat in the honey and wine or Champagne if using, and remove from the heat.

Beat the egg whites in another bowl until they hold stiff peaks.

Gently fold the beaten whites into the warm yolk mixture until blended. Divide between the gratin dishes, spreading evenly to cover the fruit. Lightly sprinkle the top of each with a dusting of icing/confectioners' sugar (this will help it to colour nicely). Cook under the hot grill/broiler for 1–2 minutes, until just browned (watch carefully because they will colour quite quickly). Serve immediately.

*VARIATION Use fresh berries when in season. Raspberries and strawberries are best, mixed or on their own.

A lot of fuss is made about making soufflés, but it's really not that complicated. The main mixture can be prepared ahead of time, leaving you with nothing more than whisking/beating egg whites and baking just before serving. It will inevitably fall as it cools, or when you stick a spoon in it, but this doesn't affect the taste in the slightest.

Vanilla orange soufflé Soufflé au vanille et à l'orange

250 ml/1 cup whole milk

1 vanilla pod/bean, split lengthways with a small sharp knife

1 tablespoon freshly grated orange zest

4 large egg yolks and 6 egg whites

100 g/½ cup caster/superfine sugar

3 tablespoons plain/all-purpose flour

1 tablespoon Grand Marnier liqueur (optional)

a deep soufflé dish, about 16 cm/ 6½ inches diameter, buttered and dusted with icing/ confectioners' sugar

Serves 4

Put the milk and vanilla pod/bean in a saucepan set over medium heat. Bring just to the boil, then cover and set aside to infuse for 15 minutes.

Put the orange zest, egg yolks and all but 1 tablespoon of the sugar in a large bowl and whisk/beat until slightly thickened and a paler yellow. Whisk/beat in the flour and the Grand Marnier, if using.

Scrape the vanilla seeds into the milk, then discard the pod/bean. Gradually whisk/beat the hot milk into the yolk mixture, then return to the saucepan and set over low heat. Cook for 2–3 minutes, stirring constantly with a wooden spoon, until thick enough to coat the back of the spoon. Let cool. (The recipe can be made up to 24 hours in advance to this stage, then cover and refrigerate until needed.)

Preheat the oven to 200°C (400°F) Gas 6.

Put the egg whites and remaining sugar in a separate bowl and beat until firm and glossy. Fold one-third of the egg whites into the cooled orange mixture until blended, then carefully but thoroughly fold in the rest.

Reduce the oven temperature to 180°C (350°F) Gas 4. Transfer the mixture to the prepared dish. Bake in the preheated oven for 20–30 minutes, until puffed. Serve immediately.

Chocolate and hazelnut soufflé cakes

Gâteaux moelleux au chocolat et aux noisettes

Though this recipe does require several mixing bowls, it is very easy to prepare. The effort will be worthwhile – these luscious little cakes are gooey and chocolatey and the perfect end to an elegant meal. Serve straight from the ramekins, pass around something creamy to pour or dollop, and enjoy!

100 g/3½ oz. dark/bittersweet chocolate, finely chopped

100 g/7 tablespoons unsalted butter, cut into pieces

2 tablespoons runny honey

3 eggs, separated

100 g/½ cup caster/superfine sugar

50 g/6 tablespoons plain/all-purpose flour

a pinch of fine sea salt

50 g/⅓ cup whole blanched hazelnuts, finely ground

whipped cream, double/heavy cream or sweetened crème fraîche, to serve

6 ramekins

Makes 6

Put the chocolate in a microwave-proof bowl and melt in the microwave on HIGH for 40 seconds. Remove, stir and repeat until almost completely melted. Remove and stir in the butter and honey. Set aside.

Put the egg whites and 1 tablespoon of the sugar in another bowl and beat until firm peaks form. Set aside.

Put the egg yolks and remaining sugar in a third bowl and beat until slightly thickened and a paler yellow. Using a spatula, fold in the flour and salt. Mix in the nuts. Add one-third of the beaten whites and mix until no streaks of white remain.

Gently fold in the remaining whites, blending well, but taking care not to overmix or you will deflate all the whites.

Preheat the oven to 180°C (350°F) Gas 4. Divide the mixture between the ramekins. Set the ramekins on a baking sheet and transfer to the preheated oven. Bake for 12–15 minutes, until just puffed and set but still jiggly in the middle. Serve warm with the cream of your choice.

*NOTE If you don't have a microwave, put the chocolate in a bowl over a saucepan of simmering water – don't let the water touch the bottom of the bowl. Leave until melted, stirring occasionally.

Rhubarb clafoutis

Clafoutis à la rhubarbe

Clafoutis, a custard-like batter baked with whole cherries, is a speciality of the Limousin region. It is one of the finest French desserts and easy to make. The only drawback is that the cherry season is a short one. Plums, pears and apples work well as substitutes, but rhubarb is fantastic, almost better than the original.

500 g/1 lb. fresh rhubarb, cut into
    3-cm/1-inch slices

200 ml/¾ cup whole milk

200 ml/¾ cup double/heavy cream

3 eggs

150 g/¾ cup sugar

¼ teaspoon ground cinnamon

a pinch of salt

1 vanilla pod/bean, split lengthways with
    a small sharp knife

50 g/6 tablespoons plain/all-purpose flour

*a baking dish, about 30 cm/12 inches diameter,
    greased with butter and sprinkled with sugar*

Serves 6

Bring a large saucepan/pot of water to the boil, add the rhubarb and cook for 2 minutes, just to blanch. Drain and set aside.

Put the milk, cream, eggs, sugar, cinnamon and salt in a bowl and mix well. Using the tip of the knife, scrape the vanilla seeds into the mixture. Add the flour and whisk/beat well.

Preheat the oven to 200°C (400°F) Gas 6. Arrange the rhubarb in the prepared baking dish. Pour the batter over the top and bake in the preheated oven for 40–45 minutes, until puffed and golden.

Tarte tatin Tarte des demoiselles tatin

An absolute French classic, this is a lot easier to make at home than you might think. You should invest in a tarte tatin pan because an ordinary cake or tart pan is not suitable. Once you make and taste this, you will come back to it time and time again, so the investment will be more than worthwhile. Crème fraîche is the authentic and best accompaniment, but simple double/heavy cream, whipped cream or even vanilla ice cream are all perfectly good.

1.5 kg/3½ lbs. apples (about 9), Golden Delicious or tart apples such as Cox

150 g/1 stick plus 2 tablespoons unsalted butter

150 g/¾ cup caster/superfine sugar

Sweet pastry / Pâte brisée

200 g/1½ cups plain/all-purpose flour

2 teaspoons caster/superfine sugar

100 g/7 tablespoons cold unsalted butter, cut into pieces

a pinch of salt

a tarte tatin pan or round, flameproof baking dish (lined copper or enamelled cast iron is best)

Serves 8

To make the pastry, put the flour, sugar, butter and salt in a food processor and, using the pulse button, process until the butter is broken down (about 5–10 pulses). Add 3 tablespoons cold water and pulse just until the dough forms coarse crumbs; add 1 more tablespoon water if necessary, but do not do more than 10 pulses. Transfer the pastry to a sheet of baking parchment, form into a ball and flatten to a disc. Wrap up in the paper and let stand for 30–60 minutes.

Roll out the pastry to a disc the diameter of the pan; turn the pan upside down on the rolled out pastry, press down and trace around the edge with the tip of a sharp knife. Transfer the pastry round to a baking sheet and chill until needed.

Peel, core and quarter the apples. Set aside.

Put the butter and sugar in the baking pan and melt over high heat, stirring to blend. Remove from the heat and arrange the apples in the pan in two circles. The inner circle should go in the opposite direction to the outer one.

Return to the heat and cook for 30 minutes. From this point, watch the apples carefully and cook for a further 5–15 minutes, until the liquid thickens and turns a golden caramel colour. Remove from the heat and put the disc of pastry on top, gently tucking in the edges.

Preheat the oven to 200°C (400°F) Gas 6. Transfer the tart to the preheated oven and bake for 45–60 minutes, until browned. Remove from the oven and let cool slightly. Invert onto a serving plate while still warm (or the caramel will harden, making it too difficult). Serve hot, warm or at room temperature.

Simple apple tart   Tarte aux pommes

Golden Delicious is the apple of preference for most French dishes. It's not an especially interesting eating variety, but it's perfect for baking and cooking. It holds its shape well and is not too tart. The vanilla-scented purée is an extra, but well worth the effort for the indulgence.

1 recipe Sweet Pastry
  (see page 140), chilled

Apple purée

3 Golden Delicious apples,
  peeled and chopped

1 vanilla pod/bean, split
  lengthways with a small
  sharp knife

2 tablespoons sugar

10 g/1 tablespoon unsalted butter

Apple topping

3 Golden Delicious apples,
  peeled and sliced

15 g/1 tablespoon unsalted butter,
  melted

1 tablespoon sugar

*baking parchment and baking
  weights or dried beans*

*a loose-based tart pan, 23–25 cm/
  9–10 inches diameter, greased
  and floured*

Serves 6

Roll out the pastry on a floured work surface to a disc slightly larger than the tart pan. Carefully transfer the pastry to the pan, patching any holes as you go and pressing gently into the sides. To trim the edges, roll a rolling pin over the top, using the edge of the pan as a cutting surface, and letting the excess fall away. Tidy up the edges and refrigerate for about 30–60 minutes, until firm.

Preheat the oven to 200°C (400°F) Gas 6. Prick the pastry all over, line with baking parchment and fill with baking weights. Bake in the preheated oven for 15 minutes, then remove the paper and weights and bake for 10–15 minutes more, until just golden. Let the tart shell cool slightly before filling.

For the apple purée, put the apples, vanilla pod/bean, sugar and butter in a saucepan, add 4 tablespoons water and cook gently for about 10–15 minutes, stirring often until soft, adding more water if necessary. Use the tip of a small knife to scrape the seeds from the vanilla pod/bean into the purée, then discard the pod/bean. Transfer the mixture to a food processor or blender and purée.

Preheat the oven to 200°C (400°F) Gas 6. Spread the purée evenly in the cooled tart shell. Arrange the apple slices in a circle around the edge; they should be slightly overlapping but not completely squashed together. Repeat for an inner circle, trimming the slices slightly so they fit, and going in the opposite direction to the outer circle.

Brush with melted butter and sprinkle with sugar. Bake in the preheated oven for about 25–35 minutes, until browned and the apples are tender. Serve warm or at room temperature.

Pear and almond tart

Tarte aux poires frangipane

This is very elegant, both in appearance and flavour. It is ideal for entertaining since the tart shell and almond cream can be made a few hours in advance. To make it even more special, serve with crème fraîche sweetened with some caster/superfine sugar, or good quality vanilla ice cream.

1 pre-baked Sweet Pastry tart shell, still in its pan and cooled (see page 142)

3–4 ripe pears*

Almond cream

100 g/7 tablespoons unsalted butter

100 g/½ cup sugar

2 eggs

100 g/½ cup ground almonds

2 tablespoons plain/all-purpose flour

baking parchment and baking weights or dried beans

a loose-based tart pan, 23–25 cm/ 9–10 inches diameter, greased and floured

Serves 6

To make the almond cream, put the butter and sugar in a bowl and beat with an electric mixer until fluffy and lemon-coloured. Beat in the eggs, one at a time. Using a spatula, fold in the almonds and flour until well mixed.

Preheat the oven to 190°C (375°F) Gas 5.

Spread the almond cream evenly in the tart shell.

Peel and slice the pears, into 8 or 12 slices, depending on the size of the pears. Arrange the pear slices on top of the almond cream.

Bake in the preheated oven for about 20–25 minutes, until puffed and golden. Serve warm.

*Note If only unripe pears are available, poach them for 5 minutes in a saucepan of water with the freshly squeezed juice of ½ a lemon.

Fresh fruit tart Tarte aux fruits frais

In French pastry shops, this tart is often made in a more orderly fashion, with all the fruit arranged in neat circles. I find it is prettier – and more accessible for the home cook – to use the higgledy-piggledy approach to fruit distribution. You can pile it as high as you like, but be warned that it can get a bit messy when serving. This does not in any way affect the taste.

1 pre-baked Sweet Pastry tart shell, still in its pan and cooled (see page 142)

Pastry cream

300 ml/1¼ cups whole milk (or half milk and half cream)

1 vanilla pod/bean, split

2 egg yolks

50 g/¼ cup caster/superfine sugar

40 g/heaping ¼ cup plain/all-purpose flour

Fruit filling

1 small punnet/basket blackberries

1 small punnet/basket blueberries

1 small punnet/basket strawberries

1 peach, thinly sliced

1 nectarine, thinly sliced

2 purple plums, thinly sliced

1 kiwi fruit, peeled, halved and thinly sliced

about 150 g/½ cup apricot jam/jelly

baking parchment and baking weights or dried beans

a loose-based tart pan, 23–25 cm/ 9–10 inches diameter, greased and floured

Serves 4—6

To make the pastry cream put the milk and vanilla pod/bean in a heavy saucepan and bring just to the boil. Remove from the heat, cover and leave to infuse for 15 minutes.

Put the egg yolks and sugar in a heatproof bowl and whisk/beat well. Whisk/beat in a bit of the hot milk to warm the yolks slowly, then add the flour and mix well. Add the remaining milk to the yolk mixture and whisk/beat until smooth. Return to the saucepan and continue cooking, stirring constantly over low heat for 2 minutes, until the mixture boils, then boil for 1 minute to thicken. Transfer to a shallow bowl, cover with baking parchment to prevent a skin forming and leave to cool. (This can be prepared up to 1 day in advance if covered and refrigerated. Whisk to loosen before using.)

Spread the pastry cream in an even layer in the cooled tart shell. Arrange the fruit on top. I start with one kind, using almost all of it, and then go on to another, until I've used all the types. Then I go back and fill in the holes with the remaining pieces.

Melt the jam/jelly and 2 tablespoons water in a small saucepan set over low heat. Strain to remove all the lumpy bits. Using a pastry brush, carefully but generously dab or brush the jam/jelly over the fruit to form a shiny glaze. Let cool. Refrigerate for 6–8 hours in advance, but return to almost room temperature to serve.

*VARIATION For a fresh strawberry tart, use 2–3 large punnets/baskets of washed and dried strawberries, halved and/or sliced depending on size. Glaze with redcurrant jam/jelly instead of apricot jam/jelly – it shouldn't need straining.

Baked fruit and custard tart

Tarte aux fruits alsacienne

Almost any fruit can be used for this recipe, which is Alsatian in origin. Plums are especially nice and any variety will do; it's even nicer if you mix yellow and purple plums. Whatever fruit you choose, the amount does depend on the size, but use the weight as a rough guide and allow a bit more, just in case. Try this with peaches, apricots, nectarines, rhubarb or apples too.

1 pre-baked Sweet Pastry tart shell, still in its pan (see page 142), baked in a round or rectangular tart pan and cooled

Tart filling

7–8 plums, about 700–800 g/ 1½–2 lbs., just ripe but not too soft

2 large eggs

6 tablespoons double/heavy cream

6 tablespoons caster/superfine sugar, plus more for sprinkling

Serves 6

For filling, quarter the plums and remove the stones. Arrange the plums in the tart shell in two circles if using a round tart pan, or in lines if using a rectangular pan. If using a round pan, the inner circle should go in the opposite direction from the outer one.

Preheat the oven to 200°C (400°F) Gas 6.

Put the eggs, cream and sugar in a large bowl and whisk/beat well. Set the tart shell carefully on a baking sheet and pour the egg mixture over the fruit, taking care to fill the tart evenly.

Transfer to the preheated oven and bake for 35–45 minutes, until puffed, just set and beginning to turn golden brown.

Remove from the oven. Sprinkle generously with sugar and serve warm or at room temperature.

I must have made a thousand lemon tarts in my day, but I really struggled to get this good enough to publish. The key lessons learned from my mistakes are these. The oven temperature must not be too high or the mixture will curdle unattractively. You really must fill the tart shell on the pulled-out oven shelf; it should be filled right to the top and no one could possibly transfer from counter to oven without spilling. And try not to do too many other things whilst baking.

Lemon tart Tarte au citron

1 pre-baked Sweet Pastry tart shell,
   still in its pan and cooled
   (see page 142)
icing/confectioners' sugar, to dust

Lemon filling

3 lemons
200 g/1 cup caster/superfine sugar
2 large whole eggs and
   2 egg yolks
100 ml/⅓ cup plus 1 tablespoon
   double/heavy cream

*baking parchment and baking
   weights or dried beans*
*a loose-based tart pan, 23–25 cm/
   9–10 inches diameter, greased
   and floured*

Serves 10

Preheat the oven to 150°C (300°F) Gas 2.

To make the filling, squeeze the juice from the lemons and strain into a bowl.

Add the sugar, eggs and egg yolks to the bowl and whisk/beat just enough to blend in the eggs. Do not whisk/beat too vigorously or the mixture will be too frothy. Stir in the cream.

Put the cooled tart shell on a baking sheet and set this on the oven rack, partly pulled out. Pour the lemon mixture through a sieve/strainer directly into the tart shell and carefully slide the oven shelf back into place. Alternatively, strain the mixture into a jug/pitcher, then pour it into the tart shell before sliding the shelf into the oven. Bake in the preheated oven for 20–25 minutes, until just set. Let cool.

Dust with icing/confectioners' sugar. Serve immediately at room temperature.

A very simple and elegant tart recipe. The chestnut flavour is subtle but quite pleasant, and it makes the texture much creamier and smoother. This can easily be made in advance and kept in the refrigerator until needed (for up to 24 hours), but do not serve it chilled; room temperature is ideal.

Chocolate chestnut tart Tarte au chocolat et aux marrons

1 pre-baked Sweet Pastry tart shell, still in its pan and cooled (see page 142)

cocoa powder, for dusting

whipped cream or sweetened crème fraîche, to serve

Chocolate chestnut filling

100 g/4 oz. dark/bittersweet chocolate, finely chopped

3 tablespoons unsalted butter

1 large egg, beaten

200 ml/¾ cup double/heavy cream

200 g/1 cup canned sweetened chestnut purée

baking parchment and baking weights or dried beans

a loose-based tart pan, 23–25 cm/ 9–10 inches diameter, greased and floured

Serves 4—6

Preheat the oven to 150°C (300°F) Gas 2.

To make the filling, put the chocolate in a large microwave-proof bowl and microwave on HIGH for 30 seconds. Remove, stir and repeat until almost completely melted. Remove, add the butter and stir until melted.

Stir in the egg, cream and chestnut purée and mix just to blend.

Put the tart shell on a baking sheet and set this on the oven rack, partly pulled out. (If you try to fill the shell and then transfer it to the oven, it will surely spill over the edges and burn.) Pour the chocolate mixture into the tart shell and carefully slide the oven shelf back into place.

Bake in the preheated oven for 20–25 minutes, until just set. Let cool to room temperature before serving.

*NOTE If you don't have a microwave, put the chocolate in a bowl over a saucepan of simmering water – don't let the water touch the bottom of the bowl. Leave until melted, stirring occasionally.

Walnut cake Gâteau aux noix

Walnuts figure prominently in the cuisine of the south-west, though I would say this is a traditional all-over-France sort of dessert. It is formal and elegant, but not too fussy. Just the right thing to finish off a Sunday lunch. It is equally nice with a cup of tea and some friendly afternoon chat. This cake keeps well, too, so you can make it a day or two in advance.

200 g/1 stick plus 6 tablespoons unsalted butter, softened

200 g/1 cup sugar

1 vanilla pod/bean, split lengthways with a small sharp knife

4 large eggs

200 g/1½ cups plain/all-purpose flour

125 g/1 cup walnut pieces, ground

walnut halves, to decorate

Caramel icing

100 g/½ cup caster/superfine sugar

a squeeze of fresh lemon juice

150 ml/⅔ cup double/heavy cream

a cake pan, 22 cm/9 inches diameter, greased

Serves 6—8

Preheat the oven to 200°C (400°F) Gas 6.

Put the butter and sugar in a large bowl and beat until fluffy. Using the tip of the knife, scrape in the vanilla seeds. Add the eggs one at a time, beating well after each addition. Using a spatula, gently fold in the flour and ground walnuts. Transfer to the prepared cake pan.

Bake in the preheated oven for 25–35 minutes, until browned and a knife inserted in the middle comes out clean. Let cool slightly, then unmould while still warm.

To make the caramel icing, put the sugar, lemon juice and 3 tablespoons water in a heavy saucepan and cook, stirring, until it turns a light caramel colour. Carefully add the cream (it can splatter), stirring until blended.

Put the cake on a wire rack set over a baking sheet to catch the drips. Pour over the icing in a thin, even layer. Decorate with walnut halves and leave for at least 2–3 hours, until the icing has set.

This traditional recipe is simplicity itself to bake. The yoghurt pot is the measure, so it doesn't really matter what size – or flavour – you use, but natural, set yoghurt is my preference. If you don't fancy the orange, try other flavourings: cinnamon, honey, vanilla, chocolate, fresh or dried fruit pieces – all work very well indeed. This is great fun to make with children.

Yoghurt cake Gâteau au yaourt

125 g/½ cup natural/plain set yoghurt

2 pots/1 cup sugar

3 pots/1½ cups plain/all-purpose flour

2 eggs

1 tablespoon sunflower oil

1 teaspoon bicarbonate of/baking soda

a pinch of salt

freshly squeezed juice of 1 orange

1 tablespoon icing/confectioners' sugar, to decorate

a deep-sided cake pan, 23 cm/ 9 inches diameter, greased

Serves 8

Preheat the oven to 180°C (350°F) Gas 4.

Empty the yoghurt into a large bowl and wipe out the pot so when you measure the other ingredients, they won't stick. Add the sugar, flour, eggs, oil, bicarbonate of soda, salt and half the orange juice. Stir well.

Pour the mixture into the prepared cake pan and bake in the preheated oven for 15–20 minutes, until a knife inserted in the middle comes out clean. Remove from the oven and pierce a few holes in the top of the cake with a fork. Pour over the remaining orange juice. Let cool slightly, then turn out onto a wire rack to cool.

To decorate, put the icing/confectioners' sugar in a sieve/strainer and hold it over the cake. Tap the edge of the sieve/strainer to release the sugar, moving around the surface to coat. A very light dusting is sufficient. Serve at room temperature.

Index

index 159

Photography credits

Key: a=above, b=below, r=right, l=left, c=centre.

Martin Brigdale
Endpapers, pages 10, 11, 13, 14, 16, 17, 18, 22, 23, 25, 26, 29, 32, 36, 39, 41–46, 49, 50, 53, 54, 57, 61, 63, 64, 67, 68, 70, 72, 74, 76, 77,78, 80, 81 inset, 82, 83, 84, 89, 90, 92, 95, 96, 98, 100, 102, 105, 107, 109, 111al, 111br, 112r, 113, 114, 116, 119, 122a, 123, 124, 128–137, 139, 141, 143, 145, 147, 149, 150, 152, 155, 156, 160.

Peter Cassidy
Pages 3, 15, 24, 27, 30, 40, 48, 56 both, 65 both, 66, 85, 88, 106, 111ar, 111bl, 112l, 117, 120, 125, 126, 127, 140, 153: Pages 2, 8, 108, 122b La Mas del la Rose, designed by Enrica Stabile.

Christopher Drake
Pages 34: Florence and Pierre Pallardy, Domaine de la Baronnie, Saint-Martin de Ré; 51, 58: interior designer Carole Oulhen; 71: family home near Aix-en-Provence with interior design by Daisy Simon (daisy.simonaix@wanadoo.fr); 115: Mireille and Jean Claude Lothon, La Cour Beaudeval Antiquities, 4 rue des Fontaines, 28210 Faverolles; 144, 148 the Chateau de Gignac, Gignac en Provence 84400 France; 157 Annie-Camille Kuentzmann-Levet Décoration

Richard Jung
Pages 31, 91, 138

Paul Massey
Page 79: Cote Jardin boutique (Place du Marche, 17590 Ars En Re, France)

© Steve Painter
Pages 1, 4, 5, 6, 7, 9, 21, 35, 59, 75, 81 background, 87, 93, 99, 103, 118, 121

Claire Richardson
Page 104: Richard Goullet, décorateur (www.richardgoullet-decoration.com, richardgoullet@gmail.com);
Page 151: Josephine Ryan Antiques (www.josephineryanantiques.co.uk)

Fritz von der Schulenburg
Page 60: Irene & Giorgio Silvagni's house in Provence

Yuki Sugiura
Page 20

Kate Whitaker
Pages 12, 28

Polly Wreford
Page 86: the home of stylist Twig Hutchinson in London (www.twighutchinson.com)